THE
STANDARD BEARER

Apostle William O. Epps Jr.

Order this book online at www.trafford.com
or email orders@trafford.com

Most Trafford titles are also available at major online book retailers.

Print information available on the last page.

ISBN: 978-1-4269-6818-1 (sc)
ISBN: 978-1-4269-6819-8 (e)

Library of Congress Control Number: 2011907040

Trafford rev. 10/23/2020

www.trafford.com
North America & international
toll-free: 844-688-6899 (USA & Canada)
fax: 812 355 4082

Contents

FOREWORD

It is an honor to submit the forward to this spiritual work, "The Standard Bearer." Apostle Epps has given a gift to the Body of Christ that is a fitting and timely message. While reading the Standard Bearer, I found it aroused in me a desire to move up higher, as well as examine my character and position in the Body of Christ. He breaks down twelve areas that a Standard Bearer must consider, examine and apply himself to: time, commitment, agreement, submission, obedience, faithfulness, relationship, fellowship, unity, order, authority and power. Each of these is broken down and defined using the Hebrew and Greek text so that we have a firm and sound Biblical foundation to stand upon.

The Standard Bearer, by Apostle Epps, would help the beginning Christian set his course to be more like Christ, Who is the standard we should emulate. The more mature Christian needs to read this study in order to refresh and redirect us back to our first Love. The author pulls us away from the distractions of our busy lives and pleasures of "Churchanity." Introspection and self examination are good for the soul, and necessary for maturity. Though the book is easy to read, it is not boring, as you can hear the voice of this great preacher depositing words of explanation and exhortation that will thunder into your heart. He draws a picture of the Father, Holy Spirit, and Son with Scriptural clarity. This makes it possible for us to know the standard we should be bearing, and he tells us what to focus upon and how to become an End Times Standard Bearer for Christ.

Carrying the Standard and respectfully submitted, Senior Pastor Don Moore, BA, MA, Sociology/Psychology/Counseling

THE STANDARD BEARER

Introduction:

What is it about; the Body of Christ, that it bears the focus of the world that Christ may be set in the forefront of everything that concerns it? It is that God has a need to be seen and known in every area of creation. Yes, because of the greatness of who he is and what he has set in order from the beginning of creation; the answer of this question helps us to recognize in some form; that the God of creation has every right to expect that what he has created will bring glory and praise to his name. This is especially true in light of the fact that he is a faithful and loving God. He is the God of all righteousness and all holiness. He could not have created in mankind anything that would not have the same potential for living in righteousness and holiness as He, Himself. Mankind was created in the image and likeness of God. (Gen. 1:26)

Therefore, God knows the indwelling potential of himself in every man. It is a super-spiritual dimension of grace and faith far beyond the capability of ordinary thinking and resolve.

Yet, because he also made men with free will; He gave the ability to choose between what was corrupt and wicked, as well as that which is righteous and holy. It is a means for personal expression of choice. Everyman has the right and choice of serving Him or not.

Isa 10:17-23;

"And the light of Israel shall be for a fire, and his Holy One for a flame: and it shall burn and devour his thorns and his briers in one day; And shall consume the glory of his forest, and of his fruitful field, both soul and body: and they shall be as when a standard bearer faints. And the rest of the trees of his forest shall be few, that a child may write them. And it shall come to pass in that day, that the remnant of Israel, and such as are escaped of the house of Jacob, shall no more again stay upon him that smote them; but shall stay upon the LORD, the Holy One of Israel, in truth. The remnant shall return, even the remnant of Jacob, unto the mighty God. For though thy people Israel be as the sand of the sea, yet a remnant of them shall return: the consumption

decreed shall overflow with righteousness. For the Lord GOD of hosts shall make a consumption, even determined, in the midst of all the land;"

With this then, we see that to serve God; we are beset with HIS standard which must be adhered to in order to be pleasing in his sight. To answer the previous questions then; the Body of Christ must be in the forefront of everything that is created. It is the evidence of restoration and renewal; that presents to the world that which God intended for us at the beginning of creation. He intended that mankind would rule over everything he had created and that the glory of the living God would dwell in the earth. In this the God of heaven and earth would be glorified and it would be seen clearly, that he had established all things for his glory and for his praise. Yes beloved, there is a need for God to be seen in all his creation; not because he has to satisfy his ego or because he must simply lord over what he has created; but because HIS truth must be absolute in everything He has established, as an evidence of who he is, to and in all that he has created. He is the sovereign and matchless God. This book is designed to give us a standard whereby we can see the expression of him in character that is foundational to the faith of every believer. When we allow the Holy Spirit to process us in these areas of understanding individually and connect us corporately; there will be a mighty move of God to prove the Church in the earth as his designated authority for all things. Come now and become God's Standard Bearer in the earth and watch God demonstrate his matchless greatness through the Body of Christ.

CHAPTER ONE

THE STANDARD

There is a need in the beginning of this book to establish a parameter of definition for the word Standard and the one who carries it. So we will look at several definitions that I believe will bring clarity to the concept that we are discussing. We will start with the definition and look at the Hebrew and Greek meanings as well for the sake of additional clarity.

The first definition for the word standard is that of;

Level of quality or excellence: the level of quality or excellence attained by somebody or something

Level of quality accepted as norm: a level of quality or excellence that is accepted as the norm or by which actual attainments are judged (often used in the plural.)

We will observe in the definitions the attributes of Christ.

Isa 59:19;

> *"So shall they fear the name of the LORD from the west, and his glory from the rising of the sun. When the enemy shall come in like a flood, the Spirit of the LORD shall lift up a standard against him."*

Christ is the pattern for our living and bearing the true Standard of God. We are then set in the earth to be Christ's representatives for effective expression of His Standard. We are to show the fullness of Who He is in everything that we do. The Word of God says that:

1Jo 4:17;

> "Herein is our love made perfect, that we may have boldness in the day of judgment: because as he is, so are we in this world."

When men have come to salvation through Christ's sacrifice (without the shedding of his blood there is no remission for sins; (Heb. 9:22) there can be no standard that is greater than the one who sets the standard for all things in heaven and in earth. His standard is the norm by which all attainments will be judged. When the standard of God was corrupted in the sin of Adam; God set in motion a plan that would bring men to restoration and healing and out of spiritual collapse. The violation of the commandment of God in the disobedience of Adam; caused all of mankind to fall. So as a result of the sin, the whole of mankind could never satisfy the demand of a just God. In God's recognition of this fact; the Word of God tells us that God became the Standard for all men in Jesus Christ.

Ezekiel 22:30 says;

> "And I sought for a man among them that should make up the hedge, and stand in the gap before me for the land, that I should not destroy it: but I found none."

God was unable to find anyone who could satisfy his demand and then He showed his greatness to save and deliver us from the bondages of sin and death. In *Hebrews 10:7* the testimonial of Christ is given concerning the need for a savior.

> "Then said I, Lo, I come in the volume of the book it is written of me, to do thy will, O God."

Christ became the eternal sacrifice for sin and now the standard for our living. He was sinless and perfect in Spirit, Mind, Will and Emotions. Therefore, he was able to subdue the effects of sin and defeat death. This made Him the perfect sacrifice and redeemer for all of mankind.

The next definition for standard is:

The authorized model or unit of measurement: an authorized model used to define a unit of measurement.

In this we realize that there is only one standard authorized for the purposes of God and the establishing of his eternal will. All men must come by distinction of the Lord Jesus Christ and his saving grace. Christ alone; is the authorized model for God's righteousness in the earth.

Acts 4:12

> *"Neither is there salvation in any other; for there is no other name, under heaven given among men, whereby we must be saved."*

Now as having come to terms *with t*he issue of Jesus Christ as the standard; (we will discuss more relatively in the book later): let's now begin to look at what the Holy Spirit revealed to me as 12 components in the foundation of the Standard Bearer. We will for the sake of understanding deal with each briefly. Please recognize that there are 12 foundations in the foundations of the New Jerusalem, the Holy City of God. It is the number of apostolic authority and government. Jerusalem is the Holy City and It is the scriptural and historical dwelling place, for the presence of The Father. The foundation for the Standard Bearer is one of Apostolic and Prophetic mandate in the Body of Christ. Just as Christ began to set the Church on the foundation of the Apostles we see this wisdom revealed by the Word of God.

Eph 2:20;

> *"And are built upon the foundation of the apostles and prophets, Jesus Christ himself being the chief corner stone;*

God is not looking for a visitation with men. He is looking for a dwelling place. The Church is that dwelling place in the earth. We must have the right foundation in order to receive the depth of the glory of God; which is to be revealed in the Church. God intends to reveal the glory of the New Jerusalem; the Holy City, first in the Body of Christ as a living structure for His presence. We must be able to bear the standard of the Lord Jesus Christ in the earth. We must become the full evidence of who he is through his true lordship in us.

Jesus said in Matthew 11:29:

> *"Take my yoke upon you and learn of me; for I am meek and lowly in heart: and ye shall find rest for your souls. Vs. 30; for my yoke is easy and my burden is light."*

O' hallelujah to God for his unspeakable gift!

Let's look now at the first 3 components in the foundations of the Standard Bearer and see the requirements of the Lord Jesus Christ for our successes in Him. Let's discover together the need for our becoming able to live, in the full liberty of the risen savior. We will further discover how each of these foundations are necessary to support the other that precedes it. This is not just a work of relationship that is without merit and necessity. Each of these is the mandate of the Spirit of God for the full intent of God: to bring a far more exceeding and eternal weight of glory to the Church *(The Body of Christ)*

2 Cor. 4:17-18 says:

> *"For our light affliction which is but for a moment works for us a far more exceeding and eternal weight of glory; While we look not at the things which are seen, but at the things which are not seen: for the things which are seen are temporal; but the things which are not seen are eternal."*

So now, the work of the Holy Spirit brings us as believers, to the place of eternal glory. This will happen, as we yield to his will and allow him to build in us the correct foundations for living in complete obedience to the Lord Jesus. We discover how to live in him, and to become compliant with the work of the Holy Spirit in our hearts and minds. So our first foundation is built on the element of *TIME*.

CHAPTER TWO

"TIME"

When I began to inquire of The Lord as to why *TIME* was the first foundation; the Holy Spirit revealed to me that it was the first place of process in the life of every believer. It is the place where God has set a standard for every life. We all must come to recognize, that there is a need to be developed in the space of time that God designates for us. When we read the Word of God, we discover that God has initiated a sequence of time for all things in creation. Every Standard Bearer must know the relevance of time to their purpose and the purposes of God in the earth. In seedtime and harvest; we understand that there is a set time to it's processes in the earth. Likewise, there is the time that is given for the full and complete plan of God in each individual to be revealed and accomplished.

Ecc.3:1-2

> *"To everything there is a season, and a time to every purpose under heaven: "A time to be born, and a time to die; a time to plant, and a time to pluck up that which is planted."*

In the courses of our living; there are other sequences of purpose and circumstance which all become involved in our experience through measured time. There is a series of definitions which speak to the issue of time in the lives of men. I will take the time to discuss them in this chapter because of how God perceives the need for his people to work through time. Often, we miss the importance of time to the purposes of life as believers. We continue in our daily routines and lose sight of the urgency to live life to it's fullest potential. That is to say; there is a need to fulfill our destiny from the perspective of Christ's purposes for us.

Those who understand time equate it with money in the business sense and others who are urgent in their understanding, are concerned for experiencing life in it's entirety with diligent and meaningful pursuits.
For the believer, the Word of God says;

John 9:4

> *"we must work while it is day; for the night cometh when no man can work."*

Now the first aspect of time for discussion is the Hebrew word:

YOME: it is a word (which is defined by associated terms); such as age, chronicles, daily, continually, and birth.

Genesis 4:3 says;

> *"In process of time it came to pass, that Cain brought of the fruit of the ground an offering unto the Lord."*

It's curious that the scripture records *(chronicles)* this particular passage in regard to the events of sacrifice and Cain's failure to bring to God the offering that He required. In a specified period of time: (the time appointed of the Lord); Cain brought to God what God could not receive for sacrifice. The sacrifice failed to satisfy God's requirement. Time was involved and in this event; completely unproductive in the purpose of Cain. Cain was placed in the earth to render to God true praise and worship. His failure in the time given to him was based in a lack of trust and truthful obedience to God. Much of what we do with the time that is given to us is unproductive to the purposes of the kingdom. We further fail to see the importance of using time with the due diligence that it should command. Your time and use of time, should speak to your pursuit of purpose. This pursuit should be pursuant to the purposes of the Kingdom of God!!

The second aspect of time is PAAMAH:

this is a reference to a specific stroke of time, ie. the striking of the anvil; also, corner, order, rank, often, thrice, second, this, two, (times) even hundredfold, (now) this, once: it speaks to events plus their order and rank. They also speak to quantity and numbers of occasions or opportunity.

An example of this is found in the Word of God.

Genesis 27:36;

> *"And he said, Is not he rightfully named Jacob? For he hath supplanted me these two times; he took away my birthright and behold, now hath take away my blessing. And he said, hast thou not reserved a blessing for me?"*

This is an illustration of order being lost; (even though God intended for Jacob to have the birthright). This also is a situation of two specific occurrences in the same frame of time. Jacob was able to gain advantage, because he recognized the time and season that he was in. He received the birthright and the blessing of inheritance that belonged to the eldest son. There is then considerable disparity between the plan or God by intent and the deceptions of Jacob to take away through trickery the birthright and blessing of the first born from Esau. Yet in the final analysis, there is the revealing of *PAAMAH*. This also speaks to the specific instance when a significant change occurred in a set time. All of us at one time or another have experienced a *PAAMAH!*

I know of such a time in experiencing a dynamic change in my life. It was the striking o f the anvil so to speak. I was sitting in a rock concert in 1975 on the campus of the University of Akron. As a college student at the time; I was absorbed with doing whatever suited me and whatever the consequences, I felt that I could handle them. I was brass and indulgent to say the least. While in this concert however; I had an experience which changed my whole life dramatically. I was caught away into the Spirit Realm and I met The Lord Jesus Christ. I did not see His face but when He begin to speak to me in what appeared to me to be a transitioning from an drug induced state (marijuana) to a very sober and focused condition: I knew immediately who He was. He began to show me images of my life and what it had been to that point and how I had done things and been involved in dangerous situations where He had protected me. I begin to weep as He revealed His love for me. Then He ask me what was I going to do? I told Him that I would go to church on Sunday and give my life to Him. That was

November 7th, 1975. On that Sunday evening November 9th, I gave my life to The Lord Jesus Christ and have served Him for these 35 years since then. That was a *PAAMAH*. It was a striking of the anvil in my life, where something drastic and dramatic took place and changed me forever. We all have had them! It is the same aspect of time which took place when Peter denied the Lord 3 times before the cock crowed. (Matt. 26:34) That is to say a time where certain events have happened and can be referred to in a specific instance in *TIME*!!! Many of us know of certain and specific instances in our lives where things happened, that changed the courses of our lives or had a specific effect upon us: events that remain as a distinction which we regard as life changing. Do you remember when you had a life changing event in your life? Do you know the specific timeframe in which those events took place? These are the *PAAMAH'S* of life. Do you remember their impact upon you? God has allowed all of us to have just such events. They become significant markers to us for purpose and destiny,

Another aspect of time is *MACHAR:* this is a more prophetic term, in that it references future events; ie.

It means, Hereafter, or time to come, the morrow, or usually tomorrow. (And it shall come to pass)"

Exodus 13:14

> "And it shall be when thy son asketh thee in time to come saying; What is this? That thou shalt say to him, by strength of hand, the Lord brought us out from Egypt, from the house of bondage."

This is *TIME* that speaks to the events to come. This is the prophetic tense of those things that shall prevail. In some instances it will identify that which is already past and be a repeating of the events and times as a matter of record. Then there is that aspect of those things which are spoken and have yet to be fulfilled. This is a consistent pattern of the Word of The Lord in unveiling itself, through promises and events that are prophesied and come to fullness in a designated season according His desire.

A fourth aspect of time is *MOWADAH:*

This is a fixed time or season: it is specifically that time which refers to festivals, and conventions, convened for special purposes. It also refers to the congregation and the meeting place. It is a signal, (as appointed beforehand): place of assembly.

In *1ˢᵗ Samuel,* we see a clear evidence of this. "And the cook took up the shoulder, and that which was upon it and set it before Saul. And Samuel said;

I Sam. 9:24;

> *"Behold that which is left! Set it before thee and eat; for unto this time hath it been kept for thee since I have said, I have invited the people. So, Saul did eat with Samuel that day."*

NOTE: These are those times when the Holy Spirit impresses upon our hearts the need for a special activity and season for purposes that he imposes. They are divine celebrations, which are set with a convening of, or gathering for, timely events or occasions. It gives to us the added grace, which incorporates; the place of the event as significant with those that assemble together as well as the season. It is a Holy Ground event; and everyone there is initiated into the experience. Samuel called all Israel to the gathering to honor the King. (Saul)

Aspect number five relates to measurements of time or fixed time. The Greek word for this is *KRONOS:*

This is *calendar time.* Generally, it is the most familiar aspect of time, which most people relate to. Kronos is demonstrated daily in our living, because most people live in a twenty-four frame of reference for time. We generally expand from there; with days, weeks, months, then years: It is especially a unit of time or interval of time. Each of them has their significance, as it relates, to those things which we plan for, in our living cycles. By definition; it can speak to individual opportunity, but also delay, years old, season, space, often (times) a while.

I Pe. 1:17 says;

> *"If you call on the Father who without respect of persons judgeth according to everyman's work, pass the time of your sojourning here in fear."*

NOTE: How we relate to *KRONOS* can determine our successes, as they relate to seasons and specific opportunities in our lives. Peter says that there will be a judging of every man's work by the Father; and that we should conduct ourselves with true reverence throughout the time of our temporary residence on the earth, whether long or short. (Amp)

The last of these aspects that I wish to speak of, is that of *KAIROS*:

This is the occasions of God which are set in proper time; they are always an opportunity, (convenient) **due season. God who lives outside of time will interrupt conventional time or *KRONOS* to bring immediate consequence to issues operating in time. It is a short while or short term. Even though God works and lives outside the confines of time; everything that He does, affects time. When God brings His presence upon time: time is affected with immediate consequences based in His desire and will. His will is established based on what He said in His word and the rhema which proceeds from His mouth.** (prophetic releases of His heart) **It is important to note that what He speaks will never violate what He already said! The declarations of the Word of God are constant and consistently before Him. The times He has set are compulsive in responding in the appropriate seasons of God. They are alive with God's spirit and presence as His Word moves upon them! We find that there is an occasion in the Word of God that presents an opportunity for God to do something that would change the course of two individuals lives. It is a set time for the deliverance and healing of two demoniacs. Yet, Jesus brings a Kairos moment into effect without changing the course of other planned time.**

In Matthew 8:29 we find;

> *"And behold, they cried out, saying; What have we to do with thee, Jesus, thou son of God? Art thou come to torment us before the time?"*

Now although Jesus is come to deliver the demoniacs; (the two possessed) **he is aware; as are the demons, of a specific time of judgment which is to come. They want to know if Christ is going to act out of timing and establish a different season. Of course Jesus is not looking to do anything against that which His Father has already set in place. So then, there are times that are appointed for the Lord to act in the affairs of his people because of convenient opportunity. These are many times, the place where we see signs and miracles take place within the Body of Christ. When we understand that**

God exists outside of time and his timeless presence comes into the affairs of men who exist in time; it presents a Kairos moment. Then the processes of men are accelerated to completion. The things that we have
struggled with in process; come to an immediate end.

II Cor. 6:2 states;

> *"For he saith, I have heard thee in a time accepted, and in the day of salvation have I succoured thee; behold, now is the accepted time; now is the day of salvation."*

This is literally a time of favor for an assured work. We have witnessed this in many healings and works of blessing which manifest in the lives of God's people at different times. When we hear the messages of the gospel preached; then is the acceptable time for the wisdom of Christ to prevail in the heart of the believer. While most times we tend to believe that nothing has happened when immediate results are not visible; it is the believing that takes place in our hearts having not seen which is most important. It is a place of knowing in the believers that what the Word of God says is absolutely true whether we can see it immediately or not.

Jesus demonstrates this further, when in John 6; he sends his disciples to Capernaum and they enter a ship to go to the other side. Jesus in the late hours of the night (3am) comes to them walking on the water. They were in the midst of a storm and turbulent seas. They were still only half way across when he stepped into the ship. Vs. 21 says; that they willingly received him into the ship and immediately the ship was at the land whither they went.

It was a *Kairos Moment*. They had struggled for hours to row to the other shore. But, because of the storm and the condition of the seas; they were unable to cross to the other side. Jesus then brings an immediate change to the process that they were in, and they come to shore; simultaneous to The Lord Jesus Christ getting into the ship. This is a tremendous encouragement to the believer that God will get involved with their circumstances. They had received a word from Christ to go to the other side and Christ confirmed His desire for them with His coming in the storm to work His will in them. God, The Father has the Body of Christ set for many such events in the course of it's growth and preparation for His coming. As a true *STANDARD BEARER* we must have a hope and expectation for the immediate presence and power of God, to manifest with us. We as the sons of God should not think it strange to see and hear of the great and mighty works of Christ, being performed in the daily lives of God's people. As we begin to understand these aspects of time, we will begin to look for the specific seasons of God and His grace for us. God, The Father, has a will for every man and woman in the earth. It is the personal pleasure of each of us to seek out His expression in our daily living. God is full of wisdom and power to perform His will and to bring us into the destiny which is given to us both individually and as a corporate body of believers. We must not miss our miracles and bless the God of all righteousness for His son Jesus Christ. Hallelujah to God for this great gift!!!!!! Also, it is important to note that how we spend our time, reveals how we value life!

CHAPTER THREE

"COMMITMENT"

The second foundation in the Standard Bearer is *COMMITMENT*. The context of this particular word holds duplicity, in that it can give a very strong emphasis to negative extremes, as well as positive.

It is the Hebrew word *PAQAD;*

It means *to visit, (with friendly or hostile intent): by analysis; to oversee, muster, charge, care for, miss, deposit, against, commit, deliver, count, be empty, keep, enjoin, hurt, do judgment, make by any means, remembrance, lack or lay up.*

With this then; there is that level of grace which God the Father bestows: a grace which brings us to the responsibility for oversight of some project or purposed consideration. It is an area of responsibility which demands our focus and attention based on the authority of his Word. It is a *Call or Calling* to manifest his will in our obedience.

There are FOUR works of *COMMITMENT* and theFirst of these is *FAITH*. The Word of the Lord must be mixed with faith in order to accomplish in us the will of God. That is to say, that there must be evidence of our commitment to Christ which is active in what God said.

Heb. 4:2

> *"For unto us was the gospel preached, as well as unto them: but the word preached did not profit them, not being mixed with faith in them that heard it."*

They suffered in their wilderness because of a lack of commitment to The God of Israel in FAITH. Faith is the essential ingredient to receiving the substance of what is hoped for in God's Word.

Heb. 11:1

> *"Now faith is the substance of things hoped for, the evidence of things not seen."*

In faith then, we produce actions that are consistent with what we confess. All faith is active and aggressive to pursue the things hoped for. You can only be committed to what you believe and confess and our confession should be consistent with what we believe is the heart and mind of Christ for our life. Further, that confession should be rooted and grounded in the TRUTH of His Word. Oftentimes, we do not relate to the will of Christ for us as such, because we lack faith and confidence in His Word. The word of God says

Heb 11:6;

> *"But without faith it is impossible to please him: for he that cometh to God must believe that he is, and that he is a rewarder of them that diligently seek him."*

The people of the Lord must learn to be diligent in seeking Him. We seek Him through His word!

Therefore the Second work of *COMMITMENT* is *TRUTH*. All our commitment must be based in the truth of God's word. God watches over his WORD. This includes the word of the Lord that is active in our heart. We must commit to the truth of God. The word of God says that God desires truth in the heart of men.

Ps 51:6;

"Behold, thou desirest truth in the inward parts: and in the hidden part thou shalt make me to know wisdom."

When we crave the word of truth; it will bring us to a greater depth of commitment and establish also, a greater consistency of faith in us. Truth is one of the principle desires of The Father, to be developed in us as believers. The revelation of *TRUTH* will bring faith alive in us as we commit to the word of God. You will only have faith for what you believe to be true! Our success in life comes from the growth and steadfastness of a committed lifestyle with faith in God's word. The Third work of COMMITMENT is one of *OBEDIENCE.* There must be a willingness to obey in our heart and to commit to the word of God. That's why we must understand that obedience is centered in our will. We choose to do right or wrong. We commit by establishing *OBEDIENCE* in our will. So when, we take the truth of God's Word as the absolute rule for our living; we center that truth in our will and make a decision to obey it. We will commit to what we are willing to obey. We further realize that in the heart of man we have soul and spirit. Our spirit is born again of an incorruptible seed by the word of God.

1Pe 1:23;

"Being born again, not of corruptible seed, but of incorruptible, by the word of God, which liveth and abides forever."

Our soul however is being processed and many of the choices to be made in life are challenged by our minds, our will itself and our emotions. So a part of what must be subdued in the process of making our will conformable to the will of Christ is US! Time will not permit us to discuss these issues but know that all of us at all times; are not and will not be readily willing to do the things which the word of God says and those things in us which hinder that work are to be brought into subjection through Christ's word. The Fourth aspect of *COMMITMENT* is TIME. There are elements of time which expose us to the heart and desire of Christ. It can be Kronos as it is measured in calendar time as well as a Paamah that can cause significant and drastic changes to occur in our daily living. We must discern what aspects of time we are operating in and allow for patience and endurance to be accomplished in us. There are times which are convened for special purposes of God and are *MOWADAH.* When we allow time to be involved in the things we have committed to; it will work in us endurance, patience, and experience. This happens because we have the distinction of waiting for the times and seasons of Christ being accomplished. So we learn and develop patience in the things which be believe in the Word of God. The conditions and circumstances that we are involved with will cause us to have to stand upon God's Word for victories and blessings. These things will take time. The bible tells us to let patience have its perfect work. This is with the knowledge that our faith is being tried (1Pe. 1:3-4) and it is working patience in us.

The Final feature to *COMMITMENT* is *TRUST*. We will see this clearly when we look at the Greek definition for commitment. God brings men to levels of commitment as they learn to trust Him and reveals that whatever we trust; we will commit to. Often we see many will come to commitment, to those things which they value and believe will bring them, a desired end. The things which bring the believer to commitment are usually those things, which test us severely. We come to know the strength of those things and trust in their merit. When the Word of the Lord is at their center; we establish faith in what He said. So then, in the heart of every man, there must be some understanding of those things which are truly important to God. All commitment is a work of faith and trust. There is a basic faith issue to consider when we recognize, that without faith it is impossible to please God. So then, all the tenets of grace and truth are established in faith and faith is established in love. How marvelous are the works of God! God then knows your faith through your willingness to commit to His Word. The Word of God is always his utmost interest. He has made himself personally responsible to watch over what he said. Jesus Christ is that incarnate word; so that everything spoken about him and by him is secured in the infallible strength of God the Father. He's the sovereign God who establishes what he said. He further watches over that same Word of God alive in us. The evidence that it lives in us is shown in our focus and commitment to it. We become doers of the Word. We keep the mandate of His covenant through accepting the responsibility for what is revealed to our hearts; and then walking it out diligently.

Again the Word of God speaks of the commitment of the coming Savior when he says:

Ps. 31:5;

> *"Into thy hands I commit my Spirit; thou hast redeemed me O' Lord God of truth."*

We find in scripture the reality of the prophetic statement of King David. Jesus, when confronted with his impending death, as he stands in the Garden of Gethsemane; must decide the level of his commitment to the Father; saying;

Luke 22:42

"Father, if thou be willing, remove this cup from me; nevertheless not my will, but thine be done."

Jesus shows the level of His commitment in his obedience to the demands of His Father by accepting death as his ultimate sacrifice for the sins of all men. The people of God are confronted daily, with the need to show their faith and dedication, to the purposes of Christ, who has chosen them. Now the Greek word for *COMMITMENT is PARATITHEMI:*

To place alongside, (food, truth); implys to deposit (as a trust) for protection; allege ie. Present, set forth, commend, commit the keeping of, put forth; set before.

We see this demonstrated in the book of Luke again, in the 23 chapter and verse 46.

"And when Jesus had cried with a loud voice, he said; Father into thy hands, I commend my Spirit: and having said thus, he gave up the ghost."

Let us then, understand, that Christ's commitment to the purposes and plans of the Father, out weighed his own desire in the natural. Because of this, he is able to deposit his trust in the Father. He releases his Spirit; (gives up the ghost) because He (The Father) will raise Him from the dead.

1st Peter 2:22-23 says;

" Who did no sin, neither was guile found in his mouth; Who when he was reviled, reviled not again; when he suffered, he threatened not, but committed himself to Him that judges righteously."

Our commitment to the things of the Lord, are held in light of our belief, that he is committed to us and will be faithful to us. Every believer is called to faithful commitment, to the plan and will of Christ. The Apostle Peter then goes on to declare in

1st Peter 4:19;

"Wherefore, let them that suffer according to the will of God, commit the keeping of their souls to him in well-doing, as unto a faithful Creator."

Christ then is well able to keep that which we have committed to him, against that day!

"2Ti 1:12;

"For the which cause I also suffer these things: nevertheless I am not ashamed: for I know whom I have believed, and am persuaded that he is able to keep that which I have committed unto him against that day"

So we must understand that we will not commit to what we will not spend time with. How we spend our time reveals what we value and our commitment to it! Any man who values any particular thing in his life, will spend time with it and will be focused and committed to it with diligence. I realize particularly that golfing is one of my favorite things to do. It can be very time consuming when learned properly. The practice time and the level of skill development required to gain a measure of proficiency is demanding. There is a level of commitment that goes beyond just playing. It is at times exhilarating and frustrating when not accomplished at the level of one's desire. But like most things in life which we hope to have success in; we must spend time with it and expect that with commitment we will be successful. Our love and commitment to Christ and His Word will produce the nature and character of God Himself in us. We were created in His image and Christ redeemed us from the curse of sin and death. Yet there is a work of the Spirit of God in our hearts which will produce His character. God is committed to carrying out His will in the hearts of men. Therefore, we come to focus on His expectation for us and resolve in our hearts to remain committed and yielded to Him.

CHAPTER FOUR

"AGREEMENT"

The Third foundation is that of AGREEMENT. It is the Greek word *SUGKATATHESIS* meaning;

a disposition of sentiment, in company with, ie. accord with.

This is evident in the pronouncement of the Apostle

Paul in 2 Cor. 6:16;

> *"And what agreement hath the temple of God with idols."*

The issue of which, is his concern regarding a disposition of sentiment: that should not exist between the people of the Lord and devils. The Saints of the Most High God, must not conform with, or agree to the works of darkness. We are the light of God in the earth as we walk in agreement with His Word. Herein we have some understanding of how we should live in agreement with the Word of the Lord: that is, the Word of the Lord must become the absolute rule for our living. Without, this agreement; we become attached with the works of darkness and unbelief. Most of us acknowledge that we are not willfully engaged in pursuing the works of darkness. This is to say that if we knew many times the depth of deception that works in the earth and the effects it is having in our daily lives at times; we would be more guarded of the issues of our heart.

Pr 4:23;

"Keep thy heart with all diligence; for out of it are the issues of life."

The problem for most is one of not discerning the heart and mind of Christ for our daily living and experience with Him. We would rather believe that we are exempt from the struggles of the world and it's system against us. Yet, without the sobriety of constant agreement with the Word of God in areas of our living, which are challenged by other ideas of flesh and spirit we are hopeless. The area of our concern should be with our soul becoming conformed to the image and likeness of Christ by becoming a living expression of Him. The expression is worked in us by conformity to the truth. That calls for a refined level of agreement expressed in action that magnifies the attributes of Christ's nature. His nature is worked in us as the word becomes a living evidence of our agreement, and manifests. With this, the next Hebrew definition gives us a more prophetic insight concerning the word agreement. The word *CHOZAH*:

which means a beholder of vision; also a compact (as looked upon) with approval, prophet, seer, stargazer, agreement shows the intent of the Lord God in areas of agreement that are futuristic in content.

The prophet declares In Isaiah 28:14-15;;

"Wherefore, hear the word of the Lord, ye scornful men, that rule this people who are in Jerusalem; Because ye have said,"

"We have made a covenant with death, and with hell are we at agreement, when the overflowing scourge shall pass through, it shall not come unto us, for we have made lies our refuge, and under falsehood have we hid ourselves"

Isaiah asserts, that it is the agreement of those who are in rule at that time, with the devices of Satan to do evil; that God has spoken a word. That word which given becomes a prophetic statement of things to come that will bring an end to the works of darkness. *Vs.* 16 states;

"Therefore, thus saith the Lord God, Behold, I lay in Zion for a foundation a stone, a tested stone, a precious cornerstone, a sure foundation; he that believeth shall not make haste."

So then, because of the agreement of men; God is compelled to release a prophetic utterance that speaks of what will come for the praise of His Kingdom. Isaiah goes on in the next verses to cite the impending judgments of God. Agreement is a foundational issue to bringing the activity of God. The constant paradigm in scripture is shown in Mt 18:19;

> *"Again I say unto you, That if two of you shall agree on earth as touching anything that they shall ask, it shall be done for them of my Father which is in heaven."*

In the 11th chapter of Genesis; it is the agreement of the people that allows them to build the tower of Babel. That agreement caused the Lord to confound their language, so that they could not communicate their intent. God uses agreement to bring order and alignment with His heart and desire in the Body of Christ. This foundation must be in place, in order for the will of God to be manifest in the believer. It is both individual in terms of personal works of the Spirit of God in the believer and corporate in the purposes of Christ in the Body of Christ's believers. Again, *AGREEMENT* is the constant and essential attribute of faith. It works a foundational truth in us which makes us stable and consistent in our focus with Christ's will. Another aspect of agreement is found in the Hebrew word *MEYSHAR*:

Meaning; agreement, evenness, prosperity, concord, straightness, rectitude, equal, equity, things that are right, sweetly, upright.

The prophet Daniel gives a clear pattern for this aspect of agreement. When the Syrians and the Egyptians joined in an alliance: Daniel 11:6a;

> *"And in the end of years shall they join themselves together; for the king's daughter of the south shall come to the king of the north to make an agreement:"*

This agreement of men was to bring even-ness, and equity to their kingdoms. It was to give their kingdoms a sense of balance and security; but their allegiance did not last because of the prophetic will of God. Men may make alliances when they fail to understand that God has a plan and that He has already declared what His will shall be. Our agreements with others or the conditions of life do not dictate the will of Christ. God then speaks of our need to agree with His will as an evidence of our love and obedience. The kingdom of God suffers violence and the violent take it by force.

Mt 11:12;

"And from the days of John the Baptist until now the kingdom of heaven suffers violence, and the violent take it by force."

This will of course presupposes the will of Christ is our focus and desire of heart. God desires a heart that will be aggressive to agree with His will and desire. You cannot take what does not belong to you independent of obedience to the principles of truth that drive the kingdom of God. In that regard; what we create will not last or stand.

The final Old Testament use of word Agreement is noted in the Hebrew word *CHAZUWTH*. This word <u>means:</u>

a look, hence (fig.) striking appearance, revelation, or (by impli) compact:-agreement, notable (one), vision.

Perhaps the strength of this word is discovered in

Isaiah 28:18 saying;

"And your covenant with death shall be annulled, and your agreement with hell shall not stand; when the overflowing scourge shall pass through, then ye shall be trampled down by it."

Now, in this particular passage of scripture, we find that Ephraim's (the northern kingdom) rule over Jerusalem is brought into judgment by God. The pride and influence of Samaria over the things of God, caused them to believe that they were safe through agreements they made independent of God's sovereignty. (Their covenant with death and hell) They envisioned that they would be safe from the judgments of The Lord. Yet, the Lord prophesied that they would be destroyed by the hordes of the Assyrian army that would come as a tempest of hail and a destroying storm. Often, we make agreements with those things which fail of the grace of God. We have agendas and envision a result that precludes His truth and judgments; even covenants with death and hell. But, The Lord shows the 10 tribes; (northern kingdom) that they cannot prevent his judgments regardless of what they have imagined. Our agreements with those things which fall outside the purposes and plans of the Living God will not prevent his judgments. We must be careful what we agree with. Many times, the enemy of our soul will give us what we believe to be insights and even revelations of those things, which stir our fleshly imaginations and desires. The Word of God says that it is the lust of the flesh, and the lust of the eyes, and the pride of life. Be certain of the things that you lend your word to, and that, which you accept as your vision and revelation.

CHAPTER FIVE

"SUBMISSION"

Now, the fourth foundation attribute for our consideration is *SUBMISSION*. It is in the Hebrew *ANAH*, meaning:

looking down or browbeating; to depress. It also means to abase, self, afflict(-ion, self), chasten self, deal hardly with, defile, exercise, force, gentleness, humble, (self), submit, weaken, in any wise.

In Genesis 16:9; the angel of the Lord came to Hagar and instructs her to go back to her mistress Sarah. This word has the idea of humble submission. The key directive of submission is that of self abasement. It hinges in the will. That is; we impose this humility as an act of our own volition. Not that which is imposed by force; but that which comes as a result of our own desire to yield, for the sake of peace or mercies to be extended, that another may benefit. Hagar is instructed by the angel, to benefit Sarah with her submission in humility. This is one of the key aspects of our agreement with the Word of God. Where there is no agreement with the Word of God: there will be a lack of submission to the will and purpose of Christ. Jesus has shown his complete submission to the Father at all times. He stated that he always did the things that pleased His Father.

Joh 8:29;

"And he that sent me is with me: the Father hath not left me alone; for I do always those things that please him."

God the Father showed his reciprocation, in that he never left the son alone. Submission to the will of the Father; brings the Father's participation with us in all things. Whatever the Father will not participate in with us, will be because of our immediate breech of His purpose and will. It is not until our desire is conformed to the purpose and will of The Father, that we experience His resolve and participation together with us for His kingdoms sake. Submission brings our order and agreement to His desire and will. This assures His participation and establishes His works in us. Let's refresh our hearts and minds at this point. Remember, we will not submit to what we do not agree with. We will not agree with what we are not committed to and commit to what we will not spend time with. What we spend time with reveals our level of commitment.

Another aspect of submission is distinguished in the Hebrew word *KACHASH:*

to be untrue, in word (to lie, feign, disown) or deed (to disappoint, fail, cringe):- deceive, deny, dissemble, fail, deal falsely, be found liars, (be-) lie, lying, submit selves.

It is interesting that, there are many times in the affairs of people in the Church; when false humility and submission are revealed. This particular aspect of submission shows there are many instances, when the hearts of people are not real and genuine. I have experienced these things in setting structure inside the ministry where I serve as both an Apostle and Pastor. There have been many who said to me; Apostle I am submitted to you and the ministry. When they were given their assignments, they walked away without any regard for what they were called to and the importance in the Body of Christ of their assignment. It is much like the two sons of a certain man:

Mt 21:28-30;

"But what think ye? A certain man had two sons; and he came to the first, and said, Son, go work to day in my vineyard.

He answered and said, I will not: but afterward he repented, and went.

And he came to the second, and said likewise. And he answered and said, I go, sir: and went not.

The one son has no real desire, to submit to the purposes of his father. In the Word of God, we find a particular attitude and spirit which exists; that is at times pervasive to the Body of Christ. It is a false submission for the sake of immediate acceptance or for personal gain. It too can be to silence and appease for the sake of their own will. The scripture says in the amplified;

Psalms 18:44;

"As soon as they heard me, they obeyed me; foreigners submitted themselves cringingly and yielded feigned obedience to me."

It is a submission borne out of hypocrisy and deceit. There is an aspect of submission in the Body of Christ which pretends to love and support the vision and purpose of Christ; but is only yielded to the extent of its pretense. Those who have other agendas and initiatives are looking for the convenient and appropriate occasion to do what they desire to do.

I once had a known Prophet come to town who fellowshipped with our ministry. This particular Prophet also had a pastoral grace and was known for starting ministries in different places around the country. I have no quarrel with any of the Lord's servants but find it particularly annoying when I see deceptions come to the Household of Faith. Every service I would invite this minister to come and sit with me and participate with us in open worship as a part of the clergy. Every week he would refuse and every time the presence and power of God would manifest, he would get up and begin to walk and prophesy. This wasn't alarming because Prophets prophesy and respond to the presence and power of God by election and calling. The Spirit of God begin to stir my spirit and reveal to me that he was there to gather sheep to himself and by standing independent of the clergy and other ministers in the services, he could distinguish himself and draw attention to himself. He wasn't there to agree with the heart and will of Christ for the House of God but to show himself. When I confronted him about what his reasons and intent were for coming to the House, he was insulted and never came again. Later I discovered that he had started and ministry in the area from people he had recruited from other ministries. He didn't stay there and build them but used them for financial support. He would come to the area at certain times and gather the money and leave. His members were in airports and different places soliciting finances for the support of the ministry. He did not have a true heart and desire for the will of Christ to be manifest: only that he have pre-eminence through his own desires. When men who are in leadership or headship in ministry; forget the will of God, they will follow their own desires. They will exhibit a spirit and character opposite the heart and desires of Christ. The

Apostle John said in 3 John 9;

> *"I wrote unto the church: but Diotrephes, who loveth to have the preeminence among them, receiveth us not."*

John said that Diotrephes liked to take the lead among them and put himself first; and that he did not acknowledge his authority or any of his instructions. (amp) This is a particularly dangerous spirit, when we fail to operate in obedience and submission to the authority of Christ. To deny the authority of Christ; is to operate without submission. The Bible says; that we are to submit ourselves to each other as an evidence of Christ's love and grace upon our lives as believers. The world will know our love and commitment to one another as we submit to one another before the Lord. We must seek genuinely to yield to one another, which at time tries the patience of many of us who would do the will of Christ because we are often challenged with those who will not. Yet, it is not our task to make men obey or submit. Christ is responsible for His Church. We must submit to His wisdom and trust the Holy Spirit to conform the hearts of His people.

Ephesians 5:21 gives this instruction:

> *"Submitting yourselves one to another in the fear of God."*

James 4:7 tells us;

> "Submit yourselves therefore to God. Resist the devil, and he will flee from you."

In this is the key to our success in relationship. We must first submit to the will of Christ; and this alone,

brings us to yield to them that are around us. Submission is not blind to the flaws of others; which at times is a contention for many. God didn't call for submission for the sake of men's perfections or even abilities. He calls for submission as a point of obedience and trust in Christ. Our submission is first and foremost to Him. We trust Christ with the hearts of others. Our responsibility is to keep faithful to Christ.

Heb 12:14;

> *"Follow peace with all men, and holiness, without which no man shall see the Lord:"*

There is in this as well an element of attitude and spirit which speak to the issue of submission completely. That element is our call to have a heart of service before God and man. Often we lose focus in this area of our call to submission. The heart and desire to serve changes the equation and makes us less subject to influences that promote self will. The servants heart is one of seeking to give ones time and effort to being a blessing and not to building self image and personal will.

The final Greek definition for submission is *HUPOTASSO* meaning: to subordinate, obey, be under obedience to; Paul said to the Corinthians in 1 Cor.16:16;

> *"That ye submit yourselves unto such, and to everyone that helps with us, and labours."*

The amplified Bible says;

> *"I urge you to pay all deference to such leaders and to enlist under them and be subject to them, as well as to everyone who joins and cooperates {with you} and labors earnestly."*

So then; to be submitted holds the idea of obedience to and cooperation with another. This is keenly regarded in relationship to the Lords will being accomplished in the kingdom. We must come under authority to one another, that Christ's kingdom may be glorified. This is very apparent in the relationship of wives to their husbands. Often, the intent of the scripture is lost in this regard: firstly, the need for balance and evenness of relationship. God does not operate in a vacuum and neither should we. There must be an concord or agreement within our hearts which says; I submit to the Word of God. Our submission to one another is made strong and focused through obedience to Him first. When we commit to Him; the impact of that commitment brings us submitted to His will. So when the Word of God in Ephesians 5:22, speaks of the relationship of husband and wife; it speaks with the thought of first; submission to Jesus Christ and then to one another. How often do we see that, there are parallels in our daily living; i.e. our marriages and relationships with our children or co-workers etc.; based on our level of commitment to Him. If we are not submitted to Him; we will not be submitted to one another! When we are not submitted to Him, it is evidence of our lack of agreement with His will and desire for our lives in that particular area of disagreement and lack of submission.

CHAPTER SIX

"OBEDIENCE"

In discovering the next foundation of the Standard Bearer; it is important to note that there is a minimal experience of relationship that we can participate in. That is; you and I can never be less than obedient to the Word of God. This particular foundation brings us to a place of worship that is induced through the life that we live in celebration of Christ. That is, our obedience to him, reflects our love and desire to please Him. Jesus told his disciples;

John 14:15:

> "If you love me, keep my commandments."

This foundation is the Hebrew word *SHAMA* meaning:

to hear intelligently (often with implications of attention, obedience etc. causative to tell, etc.): attentively, call, (gather) together, carefully, certainly, consent, consider, be content, declare, diligently, discern, give ear, (cause to let, make to) hear (-ken, tell), indeed, listen, make (a) noise, (be) obedient, obey, perceive, (make a) proclaim (-ation), publish, regard, report, shew (forth) , (make a) sound, surely, tell, understand, whosoever [heareth], witness.

I have taken the time to list the whole of the Old Testament (Hebrew) definition of the word obedience, to convey a complete thought. There is a very involved thinking in this aspect of obedience to be considered here. That is, that obedience involves the ability to hear intelligently and to give our complete attention to the matter heard. Thus we come to a place of careful certainty of the things to be considered. When we hear; we then regard and give witness to those things through cheerful and diligent actions. The Word of God is the rule and source for our understanding, in giving attendance upon those things which God commands.

John 1:14;

"says that the Word became flesh and dwelt among us, and we beheld His glory:"

this makes us understand that the Word of God must become flesh in us. It is the incarnate life of Christ demonstrated through our obedience that makes and gives evidence of His image and likeness in us. Oftentimes, the people of the Lord want to debate the commandments of the Lord. Yet, our part in the process is one of consideration and perception with surety. *(we are not just hearers, but doers of the word)*

Jas 1:22; "

"But be ye doers of the word, and not hearers only, deceiving your own selves."

We know that what His Word commands is absolutely true. His Word is then mandatory. Even as God commanded Moses in Ex. 25:9 saying;

"According to all that I show thee, after the pattern of the tabernacle, and the pattern of all the furnishings thereof, even so shall ye make it."

This is to say that we must do according to all that the Lord commands. The Word of God is the pattern and It is not optional, in regard to righteousness and true holiness. To stand in right relationship with the Father; we <u>must</u> keep his commandments. In this, we know that the Body of Christ is being built according to the pattern laid out in the Son of God.

I Peter 2:21 tells us;

"For even hereunto were ye called, because Christ also suffered for us, leaving us an example; that ye should follow in his steps."

We can be no less than what he said and what he did. When we review the Greek term for obedience; *HUPAKOE;*

We can see the call to attentive hearkening, compliance or submission, obey (ing) obedience.

God expects the people of the Lord to listen to and do what he commands. There can never be any pleasing of the Lord our God without obedience. Again, the Apostle

Paul writes in Romans 5:19;

> *"For as by one man's disobedience many were made sinners, so by the obedience of one shall many be made righteous."*

This becomes the focal point of all obedience to the will of the Lord Jesus Christ; in that he is completely obedient to the will of His Father. The church is commanded to do the same and it is given this instruction:

Revelation 2:29:

> *"He that hath an ear, let him hear what the Spirit says unto the church."*

A big part of the deception that the adversary brings against the Body of Christ is one of obstructing the ability of the believer to hear and obey what the Spirit of God is saying. The key to our becoming mature and able to be Standard Bearers of Christ in the earth; is one of *attentively hearkening (to hear and obey)* the Word of the Lord our God. There is cultivated in every believer, who will receive the instruction of the Word of God; the ability to do righteousness in every area of their life. It is not accomplished through merely knowing what the Bible says. It is done by taking that instruction as the rule for our action or response to Him. (*a doer of the Word*) In this, our response to what Christ commands is the key. It is the key because of our soul being centered in our heart. The soul then being comprised of mind, will, and emotions is challenged to submit to the obedience of Christ continually. What I am saying is we cannot respond in what we have been instructed to do absent of our treasures. Our treasures are those things which are seated in our heart. (soul) The Word of God says;

Matthew 6:2;

"For where your treasure is, there will your heart be also."

Our best treasure are greatly challenged with the ability to hear in our hearts, the voice of the Living God and respond to his desires.

In Rev. 3:6 we find;

"He that hath an ear, let him hear what the Spirit saith to the Churches."

The Amplified version says;

"He who is able to hear, let him listen to and heed what the [Holy] Spirit says to the assemblies." (Church).

Can we do any less than what is given as the directive of God particularly, as it relates to our complete and total obedience to His Word? We find that nothing else will settle His demand upon us. The Lord Jesus Christ will expect nothing less than our complete willingness to heed His Word. Paul again speaks of the disparity between them that are against the Word of God and those who are obedient to its' commands. He says to the Romans that, they are to mark them which cause divisions and offenses contrary to the doctrine which they had learned, and to avoid them. (Rom. 16:17)

Then in verse 19 he says;

"For your obedience is come abroad unto all men: I am glad therefore on your behalf; but yet I would have you wise unto that which is good, and simple concerning evil."

Again; obedience in the Word of God has to distinguish us from everything that is contrary to the heart and purposes of Christ. We find that *the test of fellowship with Christ* is reflected through our obedience to him.

I John 1:6 says;

"If we say that we have fellowship with him, and walk in darkness, we lie, and do not the truth."

It is very interesting to note that, Christ is always the focal point for becoming The Standard Bearer. It is centered in him and we can never have a relationship with him void of obedience to his word. Equally notable then, is the development and growth we receive in the things of Christ. These things which become evident in our fellowship and obedience to Him, are measured out through the gifting and ministry which are released through His love in us. (*if you love me; keep my commandments.*) **John 14:15**

The Apostle Paul again declares; Romans 1:5;

"By whom we have received grace and apostleship, for obedience to the faith among all nations, for his name."

This is in keeping with Proverbs 18:16a that declares;

"A man's gift maketh room for him."

Our obedience to the Word of God, will establish the gift and calling of the Lord in our lives and bring us into our destiny. How complete is the mind and wisdom of the Father. He executes His purpose as we obey His Word. We should continue to remember what the Prophet

Samuel said to King Saul in 1 Sam. 15"22;

"And Samuel said, Hath the LORD as great delight in burnt offerings and sacrifices, as in obeying the voice of the LORD? Behold, to obey is better than sacrifice, and to hearken than the fat of rams?"

The need to obey the Word of God is paramount to the success of the believer. Our purpose and destiny depend on the wisdom and instruction of God's truth being manifested in our living. His Word is righteous and we are called to righteousness in every area of life. There are no exceptions to the mandate of Christ in us to perform the word of God (Himself) in us. He is the incarnate living Word of God and we experience Him as we submit to Him through His Word. We are to become as He is: the living expression of Christ's nature and attributes in this present world. Samuel further concludes;

1Sa 15:23;

"For rebellion is as the sin of witchcraft, and stubbornness is as iniquity and idolatry. Because thou hast rejected the word of the LORD, he hath also rejected thee from being king."

Firstly, this means to reject the Word of God is as witchcraft, (to serve another spirit as your god.)

Secondly, **the nature of stubbornness is iniquity and idolatry. It points to self worship and rule for ones own purposes. It also shows the hardness of the heart in the individual or persons unwilling to surrender to the Words authority.**

Thirdly, **God will reject us for rejecting His Word. The Word of God is the absolute will of God for all creation and our obedience to it is mandatory! Anything else is foolishness by comparison. We are admonished to obey the Word of God with our whole heart…. Nothing else weighs as heavily on the human will nor brings as great a delight to the heart of The Living God, as obedience to His Word! Our obedience to the Word of God will reveal our submission to the God we serve. Disobedience is a willful act of insubordination when we know what the heart and mind of Christ is. Thank God for such distinguished favor and privilege for His believers!**

CHAPTER SEVEN

"FAITHFULNESS"

There is now because of the call to obediently do the whole will of Christ; an establishing of true *FAITHFULNESS*. True Faithfulness is not merely doing or repeating the same things over and over, but it is a consistency of moral fidelity and stability in serving Christ. The Hebrew word for faithfulness is *EMMUNAH*. Let's look at this definition and contrast it with the Spirit of God's work of foundational Faithfulness being worked in us.

This word speaks of firmness, security, moral fidelity, set office, stability, steady, truth, verily.

Now Psalms 36:5 declares;

"Thy mercies, O' Lord, are in the heavens and thy faithfulness reacheth into the clouds."

God then is first in setting the faithfulness of God in the heavens and earth. We recognize His firmness in what He has established. The works of His hands are wrought with continual moral fidelity and stability. They are such because they are established by a God who cannot lie. They are worked in truth. We are the conveyors of His image and likeness in the earth. In order to convey His image and likeness; we must be loyal and faithful to walk in the truth of God. We are given the focus of being faithful to the things of integrity which speak to the greatness of the God we serve. This is a work of The Spirit of Christ producing His character in us. This is why those who serve in the counterfeit kingdom; do so with zeal and dedication. (*as they have the nature and character of their father*) They live in the immoral integrity of sin and disobedience to the things of that kingdom. If we are not faithful to the works of Christ's kingdom which are done in righteousness; then we are by default faithful to the works of devils. Jesus maintains this statement in His dealings with the religious leaders of His era. They maintain that Abraham is their father and Jesus says that their daddy is the devil.

John 8:41a;

> "*Ye do the deeds of your father.*" **(the devil)**

Now this speaks very unfavorably for those who have lost integrity with the heart and will of God; who will not serve Him with their whole hearts. The Word of the Lord shows Christ's desire for us in the 1st epistle of John.

Chapter 5 verses 4-5 reveal;

> "*For whatsoever is born of God overcomes the world: and this is the victory that overcomes the world, even our faith. Who is he that overcomes the world, but he that believes that Jesus is the Son of God.*"

Now, in this we see the expectation of the Lord Jesus Christ. It is one, of complete victory over the world. It is our faith which initiates and sustains our dominion over all the works of the flesh and all the strongholds of the adversary. There can be no ambivalence in the hearts of them that seek to do the will of Christ. Without the heart of faithfulness to the will and desire of The Lord; men will falter in their thoughts and in their attitude and actions. All of our faithfulness is born out of a heart that is obedient to the Word of God. This is the driving force of faithfulness: moral stability and a security of faith that speaks of our continued obedience in everything to God. Once we learn the way of obedience as a key foundational construct: this next foundational piece solidifies our stance in the next level: which is our bearing the standard of Christ's faithfulness. Nothing will be overcome; nor will victories be won without our ability to stay consistent and focused in the purposes of Christ. Obedience to God's word will help to establish our focus. Obedience is foundational to our faithfulness. People who live or yield to another spirit will be obedient to that spirit. (demonic influence)

Ro 6:16;

> *"Know ye not, that to whom ye yield yourselves servants to obey, his servants ye are to whom ye obey; whether of sin unto death, or of obedience unto righteousness?"*

Much more then there is a wholeheartedness which makes us faithful to carry out our assignments and to stand in hardship. It is a faithfulness of spirit, which envelopes the assurance, that we can not only win but that it is right to keep righteous covenant with God. The Standard Bearer is faithful in everything that is required of them because they love Christ and will obey Him in all that they do. Standard Bearers are those who understand and keep the conditions of the covenant of Christ. They understand that God is faithful and that we are to show the image and likeness of Him; in everything we do. It's interesting to note; that to become the expression of Christ's image and likeness; we must embrace Christ's pattern of faithfulness as the standard. The standard must be proved in us through the trial and testing we experience in life. It further suggests in our processes the faithfulness of God to us. We see the evidence of this in David's statement of God's grace:

Psalms 89:1;

> *"I will sing of the mercies of the LORD for ever: with my mouth will I make known thy faithfulness to all generations."*

While God's faithfulness is seen throughout the generations; Christ is known in the faithfulness of God's Word. The Word of God speaks of Him as the Son of God who is obedient unto death and in His resurrection restores fellowship with God the Father for all mankind. The strength of this in standard becomes one of our willingness to embrace death to our own will and desires and to take to our hearts the will of the Father. It speaks to the consistency of the Lord throughout all creation. The Word of the Lord does and will maintain the faithfulness of God by character and by witness. Therefore; there must be the same constructive pattern of that faithfulness operating in the lives of the believers. It is not just something that we do because we look for the works, to be in and of themselves; the full expression of faithfulness. It is the spirit and heart of doing in obedience to the whole Word and will of Christ; as a true evidence of His righteous desire in us. God is faithful because He is not disposed to be anything else. He can do no less than He is. Note the following passage of scripture:

Ps 89:2;

"For I have said, Mercy shall be built up for ever: thy faithfulness shalt thou establish in the very heavens."

God as a covenant God is faithful in all His workings; that is, He is a God who gives promises and instruction in relationship to His people and sets His faithfulness, as a witness to all creation of His greatness. He further establishes that His counsels of old are faithfulness and truth.

Isa 25:1;

"O LORD, thou art my God; I will exalt thee, I will praise thy name; for thou hast done wonderful things; thy counsels of old are faithfulness and truth.

Let us consider now, the dimensions of God's counsel, which bring us into clarity and understanding as it relates to the faithfulness of God.

Hebrews 6:17;

"Wherein God, willing more abundantly to shew unto the heirs of promise the immutability of his counsel, confirmed it by an oath."

Now God, in His discourse with Abraham giving him the promise; tells Abraham in the same passage of scripture that He would bless and multiply him. It further states that Abraham patiently endured and obtained the promise. Vs. 14-15 In the continuation of this foundational truth; there is a wisdom of God that unfolds to confirm the firmness, security, moral fidelity, set office, stability, steadiness and truth of God.

Heb. 6:16;

"For men verily swear by the greater: and an oath for confirmation is to them an end of all strife."

The Lord then, makes us to recognize the depth; not only of His faith, in creation of all things; but also His commitment to the establishing of every word that He has spoken; to perform it. The Word of God yet, declares of Christ:

Hebrews 1:3;

"Who being the brightness of His glory and the express image of His person, upholding all things by the word of His power, when he had by Himself purged our sins, sat down on the right hand of the Majesty on high."

This portion of the word;

"upholding all things by the word of His power,"

suggests to us, an insight into the total and complete faithfulness of God. That is to say that God keeps everything in His creation with total diligence. He is completely responsible for everything He has spoken. The Psalm writer David says:

Psalms 119:89;

"For ever, O LORD, thy word is settled in heaven."

Again this speaks of the total faithfulness of the Living God. It talks of the sovereignty of His authority over all that He has created; as well as His total faithfulness to keep and sustain that creation.

So then we must ask the question that is most significant to this issue of faithfulness. How do we come to process in God; which establishes this quickened work in us?

I believe that the people of God must 1st recognize that the sovereignty of Christ is working in them. It is processed through the willingness of their spirit to obey and to do what is endemic of the Christ nature. Jesus was and is totally obedient to the will of the Father. In that obedience; He is fully committed to the fulfilling of the Father's desire. This brings with it a complete focus in the details of the Father's heart. The Word of God says then to us in that regard;

Col 1:27;

"To whom God would make known what is the riches of the glory of this mystery among the Gentiles; which is Christ in you, the hope of glory."

Now Christ as the abiding hope of God in us; calls us to a greater attention to the details of the wisdom of God. We are to search out the mysteries which reveal the riches of the glory among the Gentiles. It is the place of relationship with Him, which demands our diligence to hear and obey. We must do so with a submitted heart and passion that cannot be denied regardless of circumstances. This is also, a love for Him; that cannot be diminished under any challenge of opposition. Faithfulness says that we will not lose focus or commitment regardless of how we are challenged in our daily living. It further maintains its drive to the completion of the assignments of God, because we love Him and will not let what he desires, fail in us. This type of spiritual faithfulness demands truth and is *steady* in everything it does. It is very essential for us to recognize the importance of being faithful. Without the spirit of faithfulness; we cannot come into the next foundation. Again, every Standard Bearer will experience the challenges of serving in Christ through hardship and struggle. It is essential to the growth and development of our relationship both with Christ and man. Often we do not realize the effects of our transition through trials and the quality of faithfulness which magnifies our spirit and intent to love and obey The true and living God. This is the foundation of true Relationship with Christ! Therefore we can conclude that the evidence of our having acquired a foundation of obedience: we will cause us to walk in faithfulness to the will of Christ in our living. That faithfulness is a commitment to and an agreement with God through submission to His Word.

Ro 10:17;

"So then faith cometh by hearing, and hearing by the word of God."

As we hear the Word of God preached and ministered to our hearts; we must embrace it in our daily living.

Ro 1:17; "For therein is the righteousness of God revealed from faith to faith: as it is written, The just shall live by faith.

Our faithfulness is a life application in submission and obedience to the Word of God. I see that conditions of life being set against a backdrop of God's Word. What

I mean by this is that everything in life is to be conformed to the authority of Christ in us. That authority is measured in the depth of truth which lives in us and our willingness to stand in conformed relationship in Christ. We are faithful to Him. It is the joy of service and relationship that glorifies the Kingdom of God. Christ in us reveals character and likeness that shows the level of our trust in Him and then our faithfulness to Him. It is also, to be searched out; (*His Word*) as a part of our commitment to Christ and fellowship with the Father. We develop faithfulness with the Word of God and embrace it as His will and desire given to us as Sons of God. Our faithfulness to Him then is diligent. *STANDARD BEARERS are FAITHFUL* in their expression of Christ in every area of their lives!

CHAPTER EIGHT

RELATIONSHIP

We have come now to the foundation of *RELATIONSHIP* which is more than just knowing someone by name. It is more than the usual familiarity of the work place or the interactions of general involvements with someone. In the Kingdom of God; It is the constant and continual caring for and taking responsibility with those you live and interact with. It commands a standard of involvement. It is an abiding communication that gives credibility to the personal involvements we make. The same is true in the context of having received Christ as Lord and Saviour. With the initial inception of receiving Him into our hearts; we come into now, the place of perpetuating relationship with Him continually. Relationship by definition is:

Firstly it is: {*A relatedness between people*}

We have relatedness to Christ. It serves first as a relationship of mutual resolve. We are sinners now become sons and He is Savior and Lord.

Ro 5:8;

> *"But God commended his love toward us, in that, while we were yet sinners, Christ died for us."*

Secondly it is a connectedness between people (particularly an emotional connection);

Finally it is *a condition involving mutual dealings between different people or parties or countries etc. kinship:*

We have kinship with Christ and our relationship is sealed through the blood and faithfulness of God. Our condition of relationship is primary to our spirit's involvement; and then as it relates to our senses and emotions or our soulish man.

Ro 8:17;

> *"And if children, then heirs; heirs of God, and joint-heirs with Christ; if so be that we suffer with him, that we may be also glorified together."*

(anthropology) relatedness or connection by blood or marriage or adoption

We are connected through the blood of Christ.

Eph 2:13;

> *"But now in Christ Jesus ye who sometimes were far off are made nigh by the blood of Christ.*

We can see in this the unfolding of a spiritual and social, intercourse; which requires participation and communication as well as the building of a partnership of sorts. It calls for an agreement to be interactive out of a set of common values and needs. It brings with it a focused commitment transcending casual acquaintance or general involvement. So then, we know that our relationship with Christ involves our relatedness together; *(according to the initial definition) by revealing certain variables which lend themselves to each other, to establish a fixed purpose and need.*

That is to say,

Firstly, that we were sinners and Christ sinless.

Secondarily, His blood in the sight of the Father, gives us the ability to become sinless. (*It satisfies the demands of a just God*)

Thirdly; Christ has now brought us through the veil of His flesh, into the Holiest of Holies where we have abiding and continual relationship with the Father.

Now, although we do not see necessarily the term relationship used in the Word of God: we do see the idea of relationship used very plainly and concisely for the purposes of this discussion. Further, these are the components that were given to me by the Holy Ghost and the scriptures that were revealed to my heart. It is not our endeavor to justify what is written here; merely to explain the revelation that God expressed to me. Having said this then; let's look at some of the texts of scripture which bring credibility to our statements.

In John 6:53-69; Jesus says to the people;

*"Verily, verily, I say unto you, except ye eat the flesh of the Son of man, and drink his blood, ye have no life in you. Whoso eats my flesh, and drinks my blood, hath eternal life; and I will raise him up at the last day; for my flesh is meat indeed and my blood is drink indeed. He that eateth my flesh, and drinks my blood, dwells in me, and I in him. As the living Father hath sent me, and I live by the Father: so he that eateth me, even he shall live by me. **This is that bread which came down from heaven: not as your fathers did eat manna, and are dead: he that eateth of this bread shall live for ever.** These things said he in the synagogue, as he taught in Capernaum. Many therefore of his disciples, when they had heard this, said, This is an hard saying; who can hear it? When Jesus knew in himself that his disciples murmured at it, he said unto them, **Does this offend you?** What and if ye shall see the Son of man ascend up where he was before? It is the spirit that quickens; the flesh profits nothing: the words that I speak unto you, they are spirit, and they are life. But there are some of you that believe not. For Jesus knew from the beginning who they were that believed not, and who should betray him. And he said, Therefore; said I unto you, that no man can come unto me, except it were given unto him of my Father. **From that time many of his disciples went back, and walked no more with him.** Then said Jesus unto the twelve, Will ye also go away? Then Simon Peter answered him, Lord, to whom shall we go? **You hast the words of eternal life.** And we believe and are sure that thou art that Christ, the Son of the living God.*

At this point we find we come to recognize the emphasis of Christ in his dialogue with the disciples. He asks them whether they would go away as the others who have turned away from Him. The issue is consistent with the need *to covet relationship with Him* as the prize investment of every believer. Often we do not value relationship experiences because of the energy and effort that are required in building lasting and beneficial relationships. As well, we think in terms of how we are more personally benefited and forget the mutual needs of others in the formed alliances. It is not only that Christ needed the relationships for His personal pleasure and enjoyment but the process of mentoring and discipleship He brings to them that would carry out His will in the earth. He knew in the purposes of His Father; that the call and assignment of God must be carried out. Then the love He held for the Father was also the catalyst for His involvement with others. Beloved; God gives us an assignment in the earth and we must be assured of the purposes of the Father for us. Our love for Him must be the emphasis for what we do. We have assignments in our relationships with people as well, and our love for the Father and His son Jesus Christ must be the reason and focus for what we do towards them. Relationships help to determine whether or not we truly love with the love which is unconditional and perfect. Christ is calling us to express Him in a full assurance of faith in the earth. That expression must be centered in love. Relationship therefore is the greatest opportunity for such expression. So then it is the desire of the Living God; to bring every believer into consistent obedient and loving relationship with Himself. That is the first and most important form of relationship. Then the second and most relevant form is our involvements with one another. Can it be said that we love God and have an enduring relationship with Him independent of our expression of love for one another. Not in the least. It is impossible to convince Jesus that we love Him without keeping His Word. The Word of God commands us to love one another. That we have relationship with Christ is evident when we treat each other with the God kind of love and care. Every believer must then, build a consistent and meaningful relationship with the Creator and then show the evidence of that relationship in their involvements with others.

1Jo 4:20;

> "If a man say, I love God, and hates his brother, he is a liar: for he that loves not his brother whom he hath seen, how can he love God whom he hath not seen?

Now let us ask the question regarding relationship that is born out of another union; namely another god. We see in John's gospel chapter 8 some issues arising in regard to the spiritual allegiances that have evolved in the name of the Living God. Jesus points out to the Jews the flagrancy of their claim in:

John 8:38;

> "*I speak what I have seen with My Father, and you do what you have seen with your father.*"

Jesus speaks of the strength of relationship and it's influence over men's lives by insisting that men will do what their fathers do. He says that, had they been Abraham's children; they would have done the things which Abraham did.
John 8:39;

> "*They answered and said to Him, "Abraham is our father." Jesus said to them, "If you were Abraham's children, you would do the works of Abraham.*

Every man is bound by the influence of what is in His heart.

Pr 23:7;

> "*For as he thinks in his heart, so is he: Eat and drink, says he to thee; but his heart is not with thee.*

Jesus raises the issues of desire to destroy Him because he spoke the truth. Every man that hates the truth will seek to kill its effectiveness and worth. Every believer will love the truth and embrace its worth.

John 8:40;

> "*But now you seek to kill Me, a Man who has told you the truth which I heard from God. Abraham did not do this.*

Furthermore, Jesus reminds them that they do the deeds of their father and they insist that they were not born of fornication. They did not understand that they had left their relationship with the true and Living God and were in relationship with another god.

John 8:41;

> "*You do the deeds of your father." Then they said to Him, We were not born of fornication; we have one Father--God.*"

Those who are born of the Father will love His Son whom he sent into the world for sin. To love Jesus Christ is synonymous with loving the Father.

John 8:42;

"Jesus said to them, "If God were your Father, you would love Me, for I proceeded forth and came from God; nor have I come of Myself, but He sent Me.

Christ then makes it clear that those who love Him are able to understand His words. Those who do not love Him are not able to listen to His words. John 8:43;

"Why do you not understand my speech? Because you are not able to listen to my word"

In John 6:63, Christ states;

"It is the spirit that quickens; the flesh profits nothing: the words that I speak unto you, they are spirit, and they are life.

Without the grace of the Spirit of God; it is impossible for the words of life to be understood or even perceived in the heart of a man. God reveals Himself to them who will open their hearts to Him and believe His words. *His words are life to the believer.*

Finally, Jesus shows them that any other father (*relationship*) other then the True and Living God is unacceptable to the terms and conditions for life. To have life; *you must have the giver of life.*
John 8:44;

"You are of your father the devil, and the desires of your father you want to do. He was a murderer from the beginning, and does not stand in the truth, because there is no truth in him. When he speaks a lie, he speaks from his own resources, for he is a liar and the father of it.

God's sovereign desire for the body of His believers; is one of establishing a true fellowship and communion with us. There can be no fellowship without relationship and no relationship without faithfulness. The need to walk in relationship with God and man are foundational to our development and communion in Christ.

CHAPTER NINE

"FELLOWSHIP"

Now the eighth component in the foundation of the Standard Bearer is that of *FELLOWSHIP* or *COMMUNION*. This being built upon relationship, as the standard for our involvement, both with Christ and with one another gives us a common bond in which to worship together. That worship is established in a synergy of the Spirit of God which allows greater aspects of effective ministry and purpose to manifest. We will speak of these things in later chapters. Yet, fellowship has significant purposes beyond its natural implications for the explosive works of faith and their manifestations.

The greek word for fellowship is *KOINONIA*. It means partnership, i.e. (literally) participation, or (social) intercourse, or (pecuniary) benefaction. It also means to communicate (-ation), communion, (contri-) distribution, fellowship.

The first aspects of this word, suggests to us that we are to come into partnership with the God of Creation. We are to participate with Him in the fulfillment of His will. It is also a type of benefaction; that is to say a mutual benefit and blessing for which we are given great promise and reward. There is with this as well a place of communion and fellowship in our expressions of faith and confidence in Him, for who He is and what He does. That communication of our thoughts and words as well as our physical actions as expressions of our love for Him compel Him to respond to us through his love and grace made visible to us by His manifestations of blessing or especially the manifestation of His *PRESENCE* with us. Our communion with the Father calls us to pursuit of Him *as the sum total of our desire and regard for who He is.*

It is in that pursuit that we discover the nature and character of God as made visible. To know Him is the task at hand and for us to have fellowship with Him becomes our burden of faith.

The Apostle Paul declared in Php 3:10;

> *"That I may know him, and the power of his resurrection, and the fellowship of his sufferings, being made conformable unto his death;*

With this then, we find that there is a clarion sound to the hearts of believers for a seeking of the Living Christ. The Apostle John writes in the epistle of John a very earnest and pointed statement of fact regarding our involvements together as sons of God.

1Jo 1:3;

> *"That which we have seen and heard declare we unto you, that ye also may have fellowship with us: and truly our fellowship is with the Father, and with his Son Jesus Christ.*

Note that much of what the enemy of our soul devises against the Body of Christ; has to do with separation and division. He seeks to destroy the communion of believers. When he can keep us from fellowship; he can then keep us from *UNITY!* God has called the people of God to a deep sense of Fellowship and Communion with Him that transcends every level of division and separation and brings a greater conformity to the purpose and will of Christ. (*Where two agree*) it is not merely what we ask as those who have needs and concerns which are personal. It is also the cry of our hearts together in agreement as one man for the express will of the Living Creator to be manifest. When fellowship that is saturated with the living expression of our worship before the presence of the Almighty God; shows the integrity of His Word expressed in our intercourse through obedience: nothing is impossible. This too, is one of the evidences of the light and fellowship that we have with the Father. Again John declares that there is fellowship one with another as we walk in the light of Christ.

1Jo 1:7;

"But if we walk in the light, as he is in the light, we have fellowship one with another, and the blood of Jesus Christ his Son cleanses us from all sin.

The evidence of our fellowship with the Father becomes expressed as we walk in the light. The areas of darkness in our soul become exposed to the truth and great change takes place in us. The evidence that the Body of Christ is walking in light will be seen when the barriers of division and separation have been torn down and the common agreement of relationship and fellowship have manifested in The Body of Christ. Christ does not care about what we confess as our love and desire for Him when we do not show by our actions the expression of His Word. The truth manifests to make us free. The polarizing effects of social prejudice and spiritual prejudice have all but crippled the Body of Christ in many places. We have had segregations of different sorts which have not only divided the Body of Christ but made stagnant the grace of God that relates to advancing the Kingdom of God. Doctrines such as water baptism and whether or not you are born again if you haven't been baptized in Jesus' name, reveal man's error in the Word of God and have divided the Body. There are divisions having to do with gifts and elections in the Church such as five-fold ministry that divide us. Racial divides have been issues concerning fellowship and true biblical relationship. Yet the Word of the Lord God is being delivered into the hearts of men and women of integrity who will carry out its mandate. God be glorified for His marvelous works among men.

Finally in this chapter we want to briefly look at how relationship and fellowship together; bring a greater depth of synergy to generations. This occurs when the wisdom of the Fathers is transferred to the sons. We look at the works of King David and the legacy that is given to his son King Solomon. The determination of King David that he would build a sanctuary for the presence of the Lord to dwell in becomes diverted, as God decides that it would be Solomon that would build His temple. David is a man of war and God says to him that he has blood on his hands. Yet with this, God has given him a promise that his lineage would always sit upon the throne forever. God makes the house of Saul barren and gives the throne to David.

2Sa 3:10;

"To translate the kingdom from the house of Saul, and to set up the throne of David over Israel and over Judah, from Dan even to Beersheba"

This is established because of Saul's failure for true relationship and communion with God the Father. Saul failed to understand that as the Captain over Israel; he bore the Standard of God for the kingdom. Saul was to be the true Standard Bearer in Israel for his generation and that which was to come. Still he desired only to live according to his own stubborn and rebellious desires. In generational terms; Sauls bloodline has a life span which is cut short because of Sauls disobedience. But, David who has true relationship and communion with the Father, then receives the kingdom. God calls David a man after His own heart. David become God's Standard Bearer because of his Fellowship and true Communion with God. True relationship and fellowship will bring the heart of God and establish the heart of God in us.

Ps 103:17;

> *"But the mercy of the LORD is from everlasting to everlasting upon them that fear him, and his righteousness unto children's children;*

Because of this fellowship and communion with God; Solomon inherits the generational blessing of his father David.

1Ki 1:37;

> *"As the LORD hath been with my lord the king, even so be he with Solomon, and make his throne greater than the throne of my lord king David.*

Christ's expectation for His people is that our sons will receive an inheritance that makes them greater than their fathers. Our relationship with our children should be great with the wisdom and knowledge and love of the Living Christ manifesting through us to them and to children's children.

Pr 13:22;

> *"A good man leaves an inheritance to his children's children: and the wealth of the sinner is laid up for the just.*

Pr 17:6;

> *"Children's children are the crown of old men; and the glory of children are their fathers.*

So just as we are called to communion and fellowship with the Father (God) through Jesus Christ His Son; so our relationships and fellowship with one another maintains certain dynamics as well. Jesus prayed:

John; 17:21

> "*that they all may be one, as You, Father, are in Me, and I in You; that they also may be one in Us, that the world may believe that You sent Me.*

John: 17:22

> "And the glory which You gave Me I have given them, that they may be one just as We are one.

Our fellowship with the Father is produced when we become one with His son and in that fellowship of faith; the glory of the Lord will come. Being one with Christ brings the Glory of God! Also, we become perfect in one, through this fellowship with the Father and Son.

John 17:22;

> "*And the glory which You gave Me I have given them, that they may be one just as We are one.*

Glory then makes us one. We must participate with the God of all righteousness and His Son, as the Holy Spirit equips us and challenges our hearts with the Word of God. (The Word will make us free) **Without the FELLOWSHIP/COMMUNION of the Spirit working in our hearts; it shows the strain of and even failure of true Relationship to be formed in The Body of Christ. Where there is no true Fellowship, there can be no UNITY! Let us participate together with Christ's heart and desire for Fellowship which is true and lasting!**

CHAPTER TEN

"UNITY"

Now isn't it curious that God has called us into fellowship of the Spirit of Christ; in order to establish our ninth component which is *UNITY* in the foundation of the Standard Bearer. The Hebrew word for unity is:

YACHAD which means properly, a unit, i.e. (adverb) unitedly:--alike, at all (once), both, likewise, only, (al-)together, withal. a primitive root; to be (or become) one:--join, unite.

As we stated in the previous chapter, the dynamics of our fellowship and communion; whether as individuals working one on one to build relationships which tender fellowship and communion or whether as a collective body: our commonality together is our salvation, which determines our passion and pursuit of Jesus Christ. Again, as we receive Christ as our Lord, we as well receive the Father in that fellowship.

John; 14:23;

> *"Jesus answered and said unto him, If a man love me, he will keep my words: and my Father will love him, and we will come unto him, and make our abode with him.*

The central theme for our unity becomes magnified in this passage of scripture. It is the promise of Christ and the Father of Glory to dwell with us and in us. The Body of Christ then is called in assignment to keep the words of Christ. It becomes the initial evidence of our love for Him. The commandments of God give us insight into the nature and character of The Father. If we will dwell with Him; we must dwell in unity and agreement. There are divisions manifest in the disobedience of believers because of petty differences and many personal agenda's.

Christ's prayer of John 17:21;

> "That they all may be one; as thou, Father, art in me, and I in thee, that they also may be one in us: that the world may believe that thou hast sent me;

This statement reveals to us how the need of the Father and of Christ requires the unity of the believers with them. If we are in Them and They in us; we are walking together in *UNITY*. The very concept of alike, which means; that which is the same, carries with it this dimension of thinking: *likewise and altogether*. Likewise, speaks of the duplication of character and characteristics.

In addition; moreover; also

Also in like manner;

While altogether, asserts that they are one in scope and purpose.

wholly; entirely; completely; quite:
with all or everything included:
with everything considered; on the whole:

It is the knitting of our hearts and minds and spirit with the heart, mind and spirit of Christ. So then we as believers, in the Lord Jesus Christ, must recognize the importance of coming to unity. It is the willful and complete expectation of our Father for the people of God.

Now the Greek word for unity is *HENOTES,* Which means oneness, i.e. unanimity: unity. The Apostle Paul in his discussion and instruction for the Church at Ephesus; tells them that the ministerial gifts of Christ were given for the specific work of ministry that would bring perfection to the Body of Christ.

Eph 4:11;

> And he gave some, apostles; and some, prophets; and some, evangelists; and some, pastors and teachers;

The First **business and purpose of 5-fold ministry gifting, is one of establishing the dominion authority of the Word of God in every area of man's living. That is to say, make the truth of God available not only in the Body of Christ but in every arena of society and culture.**

VS. 12;

> *"For the perfecting of the saints, for the work of the ministry, for the edifying of the body of Christ"*

The *Second* **aspects of these ministries; is the perfecting of the saints of God and the edifying of the Body of Christ. Christ's body should be matured and developed in the wisdom and understanding of the Word of God. This maturity then is to be seen in the daily living of the people of God. Christ's body is to be edified: meaning confirmed as a structure or building. We should note and understand that God is not looking for a visitation with the Body of Christ; but for the Body of Christ to be His dwelling place.**

VS. 13;

> *"Till we all come in the unity of the faith, and of the knowledge of the Son of God, unto a perfect man, unto the measure of the stature of the fullness of Christ:"*

This work of the Spirit of God is to bring the Body of Christ into the *UNITY* of the faith. This will only happen as the knowledge of the Son of God is made manifest in the hearts and minds of the believer. Christ is looking for the corporate agreement of the Church! The perfect or mature man will emerge to become the measure of the stature of the fullness of Christ.

O' give praise and glory to God, for His wonderful wisdom and grace! Much of the weakness in the Body of Christ is based in its lack of unity.

Eph 4:3;

"Endeavoring to keep the unity of the Spirit in the bond of peace."

Our end-time responsibility as believers compels us to seek to be unified. The Spirit also, shows us in the pattern of the Godhead, that our focus should be one of unity.

Mt 28:19;

"Go ye therefore, and teach all nations, baptizing them in the name of the Father, and of the Son, and of the Holy Ghost:"

1Jo 5:7;

"For there are three that bear record in heaven, the Father, the Word, and the Holy Ghost: and these three are one."

We are to come to unity as believers because we are the image of Christ expressed in the earth. Our differences are not to disqualify us from participating together as the Body of Christ. The Word of God records that we are members in particular.

1Co 12:27;

"Now ye are the body of Christ, and members in particular."

This statement of truth defines the relevance of purpose and unity together in the Body. We do not cut off parts of the physical body because they are different. We instead, embrace what each brings to the expression of the body as a whole. My fingers are useless when separated from the rest of my body. My toes are ineffective when removed from the rest of my body. God has given each part of the body to specific purpose and function and such is true in the Body of Christ.

Eph 4:16;

"From whom the whole body fitly joined together and compacted by that which every joint supplieth, according to the effectual working in the measure of every part, maketh increase of the body unto the edifying of itself in love."

God says that we are joined together to supply to the Body everything necessary for the successful administration of the functions of Christ. (*We are His Body*) Each part of the Body brings a different expression of Christ. We must then learn to respect and embrace what Christ has given us as essential to the total performance of the Body. Satan has manipulated the people of God through religious spirits, deceptions and confusions; as well as lies against the Believers to keep division and separation in the Body. How viable can we be as The Body of Christ when we are divided by the foolishnesses of men which work to destroy the unity of the faith? Christ is not cut up into little pieces! The Apostle Paul recognized this deception when he talked to the Corinthians about the water baptism. He said to them that their lack of understanding produced contentions among them. The body of Believers had begun to assign themselves to the various people who had baptized them as though Christ was divided into little pieces and there was a emphasis placed upon who baptized them into the faith of Christ! The same has become true now, because of denominationalism and separatist attitudes in the Body of Believers in Christ. Is Christ divided? We must ask ourselves whether this be the will of Christ! We dismiss whatever doesn't fit by color or education, or money and station. Excuses such as;

"they are not our kind, or we have the truth and no one else compares with us, or this is the only way to do what needs to be done , or it was good enough for Momma and Grand momma; it's good enough for me." (stop this foolishness)

The people of God must not live steeped in traditions and an unwillingness to change, or to be conformed to the image of Christ. It is Christ's privilege to be diverse and distinct in His Body. We are simply blessed to be a part of His gift and supply! Glory to God for what He has done! Our *UNITY* will speak very directly to the elements of truth which establish faith in the believer. What I am saying is this: the Body of Christ will manifest with Authority and power when the Communion of the Godhead is worked in us and Unity established. This will then bring the Order of God to the body!

CHAPTER ELEVEN

"ORDER"

Let us look now at the progression that we see in the Word of God for the tenth foundation in the Standard Bearer. It is needful to note that we are called now into the *ORDER* of the Spirit of God in our living. This order has to do with being challenged to make judicial judgments in our lives as they pertain to Christ's will and assignments for us. The Old Testament word for order is the word *MISHPAT.* This word means:

properly, a verdict (favorable or unfavorable) pronounced judicially, especially a sentence or formal decree (human or (participant's) divine law, individual or collective), including the act, the place, the suit, the crime, and the penalty; abstractly, justice, including a participant's right or privilege.

Recognize that a verdict is a decision made in regard to something to be decided upon whether it is judged favorably or not. It is the establishing of formal decrees and their penalties with the rights and privileges of the party in question. It is further, those decisions based in the discretion or customs of individuals making the decisions. It can show the manner and measure, ordinances and fashion of disposing of a condition or situation. Many times it is by ceremony and or style whether customary or statutory. Judgment and justice are or may be subject to all these conditions of choice when misunderstood in their context. In the will and purposes of Christ; the truest meaning is one of the intent of the Spirit of God based in what God said. It is what is right and what is to be judicially mandated by those who are making the decisions. It is to be based on God's Word as they are being directed by the Holy Spirit. Oftentimes, we see even in our worship services a lack of understanding as it relates to order. We presume that what is structured, is order in our services. The proper order of any service calls for discovering the heart of Christ and then operating in the flow of the Spirit of God as He directs. So then, the fact that we start the service at 11 am Sunday morning and have a scripture reading, then prayer for 5 minutes and then praise and worship is structure but not necessarily order if the Spirit of God is calling for confession and repentance at the altar. We must begin to change how we perceive the will of Christ by His leading and not by traditions and formality that bind the will of Christ in our ministries. Order is also, that place of operation in judicial decision, where what is right is established for the sake of justice and righteousness. This is to say that we cannot find order in what is false and inconsistent with the truth. Gods' order will always be mandated in truth. The Apostle Paul again tells the Church at Colosse;

Col 2:5;

> *"For though I be absent in the flesh, yet am I with you in the spirit, joying and beholding your order, and the steadfastness of your faith in Christ."*

Our word here for order is *TAXIS*. It means;

regular arrangement, i.e. (in time) fixed succession (of rank or character), official dignity:--order.

In this regard, we assess that there is an official position to the things of God. That position is always based in the righteousness of the Lord Jesus Christ. Nothing that is done in the name of Christ can be corrupt or evil in its intent or practice.

2Ti 2:19;

> *"Nevertheless the foundation of God stands sure, having this seal, The Lord knows them that are his. And, Let every one that names the name of Christ depart from iniquity."*

Jesus Christ is the foundation of the Church which is His body. This is the rank and character of righteousness in the believer. You are positioned in Him. We have no other dignity that fits with our position and station in Christ. Ephesians chapter one magnifies this position from the eternal perspective of God.

Eph 1:3;

"Blessed be the God and Father of our Lord Jesus Christ, who hath blessed us with all spiritual blessings in heavenly places in Christ."

Now, the arrangement of God for us in Christ is one of fixed succession in time and eternity. It has been pre-determined as the order of God for every believer that we should have the eternal benefit of salvation. This is given in Christ Jesus, that we should be holy and without blame before him in love.

Eph 1:4;

"According as he hath chosen us in him before the foundation of the world, that we should be holy and without blame before him in love:"

Eph 1:5;

"Having predestinated us unto the adoption of children by Jesus Christ to himself, according to the good pleasure of his will,"

It is already determined by the living Creator for all who believe. The importance of these things is not merely the blessedness of the salvation we receive; but the eternal order that is established in the working of His will to perform His Word. Then we conclude with this that our position in the Body of Christ will mirror the eternal order of the Living God.

Ephe. 2:6;

"And hath raised us up together, and made us sit together in heavenly places in Christ Jesus."

The strength of this word becomes shaped and fashioned in our hearts recognizing and adhering to the proper order of all things revealed by the Spirit of God. The Standard of God is already set in our positioning in the heavenlies. We are seated together in Christ and we are His *Standard Bearers* who will walk in His *ORDER*. God has already given us the position and the divine arrangement of all things spiritual. What we may lack as a body of believers can be known as we pursue Christ for wisdom and revelation and understanding in the Word of God. The Apostle James tells us that God gives wisdom liberally.

Jas 1:5;

> "If any of you lack wisdom, let him ask of God, that giveth to all men liberally, and upbraids not; and it shall be given him."

Yet, I am convinced that we as believers have enough of the wisdom and understanding of the Lord, to be tremendously effective for the sake of HIS kingdom! It is not as much as what we don't know I believe; as it is a need for the hearts of men to become determined to walk in obedience to the will of Christ and not our will as men. The Spirit of God is never out of order.

Men who will not submit to the Spirit of Christ are out of order. The proper order for all things in the kingdom, are referenced in God's Word and carried out through obedience to the Spirit of God.

There are several other things that we could discuss in this book in regard to order. The understanding of rank and position in the Body of Christ as it relates to the 5-fold ministry gifting is one subject in need of clarity in the Church. We know that the Body of Christ has attempted to perfect the Church with partial gifting and anointing. It takes all the 5-fold gifting to perfect the Body of Christ.

Eph 4:11;

> "And he gave some, apostles; and some, prophets; and some, evangelists; and some, pastors and teachers;"

Eph 4:12;

> "For the perfecting of the saints, for the work of the ministry, for the edifying of the body of Christ":

Eph 4:13;

"Till we all come in the unity of the faith, and of the knowledge of the Son of God, unto a perfect man, unto the measure of the stature of the fullness of Christ:"

This in itself is a large part of the difficulty of the Church. It speaks to several aspects of religious mindsets that exist and affect the strength of the Body of Christ because of it's reluctance to change. God makes it clear, that the Body of Christ can come into the unity of the faith and the knowledge of the Son of God, unto a perfect man; but only through the 5 ministerial gifts which Christ gave at His ascension. The fullness of the stature of Christ will be realized when the Body begins to avail itself to the whole Word of Truth. Equally as important is the ranking that the Apostle Paul speaks of in 1 Cor.12:28. He speaks to the importance of these rankings as members of the Body of Christ.

1Co 12:28;

"And God hath set some in the church, first apostles, secondarily prophets, thirdly teachers, after that miracles, then gifts of healings, helps, governments, diversities of tongues."

Exclusively, the issues of the Body of Christ are not as complex as they appear on the surface. What is paramount to every issue in the Body of Christ is its love. When the love of God is being expressed in the midst of HIS people; there is a greater desire to do what pleases Christ. Essentially, we miss it in our services and in our relationships and experiences together because our love is not perfected. Everything that God does, He does in love and we must not fail in that order of things. If we are to have the order of God in all that we do; love must come forth as our motivation for becoming ordered together. God is not angry with HIS people but He is concerned for the motivation of our hearts. Proper order in the kingdom of God is to hear and obey His Spirit in all things. We must do these things in love that is unconditional and unrelenting in it' pursuit of HIM!! Further, much of the critical struggle in the mindsets of the believer; are composed of misunderstanding. It is the misunderstanding of the importance of who Christ is and what our responsibility is to Him. We have nothing of ourselves which qualifies us in the presence of Almighty God except our *FELLOWSHIP* with The Lord Jesus Christ. Therefore, our pursuit of Christ is the essential concern. It is *ORDER* to seek after Him and to pursue Him! Many times when we come into services or gatherings; we are more focused on the persons or individuals who stand before us as the focal point for our worship experience. They may be leading out in the area of praise or worship; yet, the focus is Christ alone. While an individual may be encouraging us in the session; we are to order our hearts to render to the Living Christ, the glory and honor that is due to Him. Every worshipper's responsibility then becomes one of personal pursuit of Christ in the worship experience. Often we find that men's agendas are more important than Christ's presence. We have idols that are worshipped instead of the God we say that we love and serve. What are these idols? They are motivations and desires of hearts that look to have pre-eminence in the gatherings. This pre-eminence is for the sake of being seen and known for our spiritualism. Then men are not aware of the influence being made on the Body of Believers which caters to soulish and carnal desires. Then we are not focused on the intent and order of Christ for what He desires to accomplish in the hearts and souls of men in those times of fellowship and communion together. It affects also the works of His grace which would be given in an atmosphere of faith, where the only agenda is Him. So now as we stated concerning the *ORDER* of gifting in the Body of Christ: to be called an Apostle (sent one) but not walk in the true order of God is futile. We are as positioned in the Body of Christ, with great responsibility to lead and guide through the Holy Spirit into truth. We come to understand the Prophet's office as one who hears and sees the heart and mind of God for the people of God. The role of the Teacher as one who makes certain that the truth is kept accurate and focused in the people of God. Five-fold ministry is complementary in its every aspect. The Pastors shepherd the flocks and keep the people from wolves and snares. The heart of the Evangelist looks to advance the kingdom of God by spreading the message of the gospel. The working of miracles is also formidable in the Body for tangible evidences of God's power and love for His people. Helps and governments should the willingness of the Body of Believers to walk together in agreement in the purposes of Christ. Every part of the body has it's designated position and assignment. God be gracious to those who would turn men's hearts from the truth. As well, we must hunger and thirst for Jesus Christ not just as an individual desire; but also a corporate one. Order then speaks to the pursuit of Christ according to His leading and instruction in our hearts. We obey Him to give to Him what He requires. Order starts in our hearts as an act of *OUR* will. It is carried out in observance of the Word of Truth vested in us: both logos and rhema. How much the Father wills and desires to receive us as we honor Him through His Son! There is no conflict in our settings for worship and praise when we love Him and are seeking together to please Him. This brings us to a new dimension of co-operation and agreement because we have common purpose. Order then speaks to our commonality of interest in the pursuit of The Father through His Son Jesus

Christ. As we have stated in the previous chapters; *UNITY* is a condition of the heart which allows the *ORDER* of God to manifest and brings us to a critical area of trust. It is an area, not of our trust in Christ but His ability to trust us with HIS Authority. Therefore, let us seek Him together!

CHAPTER TWELVE

"AUTHORITY"

Can we as believers, then recognize that as *ORDER* comes to the Body of Christ; we can and will be given greater *AUTHORITY*? Much of the issue I believe for the Church as a whole, has to do with God's not being able to trust us with His authority to carry out powerful assignments of faith and dominion as a Body of Believers. We can see glimpses of tremendous authority in parts of the Body of Christ but not as a whole body. Why is this important to the Kingdom of God? This becomes an issue in terms of the kingdom because of the principles of scripture which speak to the personality of Christ as the head of the Body being manifested in every part. Psalms 133:1-3; shows us a pattern for the Body as it relates to the Order and Authority of God in His people.

Psalms 133:1-3;

> *"Behold, how good and how pleasant it is for brethren to dwell together in unity! It is like the precious ointment upon the head that ran down upon the beard, even Aaron's beard: that went down to the skirts of his garments. As the dew of Hermon, and as the dew that descended upon the mountains of Zion: for there the LORD commanded the blessing, even life for evermore."*

The *First* thing that we take note of in this passage is: the ointment is poured upon the head. This is the anointing of headship with the wisdom and authority to carry out God's will. God always sets order to what He does by making someone responsible for the assignment. *Secondly,* the ointment flows into the beard which speaks of leadership in the body. In the anointing of the headship for responsibility; God gives the wisdom and gifting to those brought under submission to the vision and plan of God to assist with that responsibility. *Thirdly,* there is the running of the ointment into the body (*skirts of the garments*) which is the people of God. The Body of Christ receives the authority to do the works of the Spirit of God. They are then released to do by common relationship and responsibility what Christ has mandated as His sovereign will. The greater saturation point for the anointing is in the skirts of the garment! This is the place where God has commanded the greater blessing. The Body of Christ is the focal point for everything that God desires to do in establishing the fullness of Christ. The fullness of Christ in the Body of Christ will bring deliverance to all creation. Everything that has been created is subject to the dominion authority of The Lord Jesus Christ. We are to be the fullness of Christ in the earth and all of creation is in anticipation of this great move of God to restore and heal His creation.

Ro 8:21;

"Because the creature itself also shall be delivered from the bondage of corruption into the glorious liberty of the children of God"

Ro 8:22;

"For we know that the whole creation groans and travails in pain together until now"

The Body of Christ then, is charged with going forth in the power of God to perform the will and function of Christ in the earth. With this, we can recognize that great transition and change must come to the Body. This changes the expectation of our hearts.

Ro 8:23;

"And not only they, but ourselves also, which have the first fruits of the Spirit, even we ourselves groan within ourselves, waiting for the adoption, to wit, the redemption of our body."

The Word of God which further expresses this change and expectation is made clear through Hebrews chapter 10 and verse 20.

"By a new and living way, which he hath consecrated for us, through the veil, that is to say, his flesh;"

This shows us that God has already made the way for us as Sons of God through the redemptive work of The Lord Jesus Christ. *It is* a new and living way. It is not through a religious spirit or legalism or any work of flesh. It is by the living Word of God being made manifest in the people of God. It will be a people fully and completely submitted to the will and desire of His heart and then motivated and empowered through Christ's authority. That authority will be given to those who love Christ and submit totally and completely to His nature and character being worked in them through truth. John the Apostle writes:

John 8:32;

"And ye shall know the truth, and the truth shall make you free."

The freedom comes through the working of His truth in the hearts of the people of God and confident faith to follow after Him obediently in all things. Authority is given out of trust and loyalty of heart to the one who gives that authority. This authority can only be received and not taken. Christ develops that trust in us by working us through life's circumstances and we are graded based on our willingness to do righteousness and live according to His standard. So the motive of our hearts is very much an issue with The Father, who measures every heart based on its intent. These matters or intents then become the place of our growth and development. The place of our weakness becomes the place of our greatest grace. Lord Jesus Christ shows us this in His statements to the Apostle Paul regarding Paul's desire to be healed of his infirmity. He tells Paul; 2Co 12:9;

"And he said unto me, My grace is sufficient for thee: for my strength is made perfect in weakness"

He develops us in these things as they relate to the character of Christ and the Kingdom of God. Therefore our development individually also manifests in the growth of the Kingdom of God. Jesus told His disciples that the kingdom of God was within them.

Lu 17:21;

"Neither shall they say, Lo here! or, lo there! for, behold, the kingdom of God is within you."

The kingdom of God within us will be exposed through His Word made alive in us. We learn and develop through the teaching and revelation we receive from Him. The engrafted Word of God which is able to change us inwardly and manifest the character of Christ is essential to the growth of the Body of Christ.

Jas 1:21;

"Wherefore lay apart all filthiness and superfluity of naughtiness, and receive with meekness the engrafted word, which is able to save your souls."

The Body of Christ is brought to maturity by process and changed into Christ's image and likeness. Our Soul becomes prosperous in the heart; (mind and will) of Christ. With this process, His authority is developed in them that believe!

Now, as Christ did everything with the complete authority of His Father.

Mt 7:29;

"For he taught them as one having authority, and not as the scribes."

He recognized that the *AUTHORITY* of His Father was given because of the position of relationship and fellowship He occupied. Not only as God The Son is this context relevant but also significant in understanding His license to give to the Church (*His Body*) that same authority as inherent. Now we recognize the *UNITY* and the *ORDER* that follows with Him to release *AUTHORITY* to the Church.

The word for *AUTHORITY* in the greek is *EXOUSIA* meaning;

privilege, force, capacity, competency, freedom, or (objectively) mastery (concretely, magistrate, superhuman, potentate, token of control), delegated influence:--authority, jurisdiction, liberty, power, right, strength.

Christ's desire for every believer is that the Kingdom of God that is within us should be advanced to the Glory and praise of His name. S0 then the authority of God in us is for the express purpose of advancing His kingdom! The Word of God reveals how wonderous God is in working in our heart the will and the desire of Christ so that the kingdom of God will be glorified. He uses us (*the foolish thing*) by taking our frailty and shortcomings and working in us His Word of truth. His Word changes our hearts and makes us fit for the kingdom purposes of Christ. Conditions of our living are challenges which become exclusive to the plans of God for His glory. He works them for our good while changing us in the process and establishes them according to His purpose.

Ro 8:28;

"And we know that all things work together for good to them that love God, to them who are the called according to his purpose."

The greater challenge for us is not that Christ isn't able to work out His Word in us. It is simply that, we must endure process and allow that the suffering of this present time will not be able to deter us from the mandate He has placed on our lives as believers. The Apostle Paul said:

Ro 8:18;

"For I reckon that the sufferings of this present time are not worthy to be compared with the glory which shall be revealed in us"

God simply wants to reveal His glory in us and give to us the authority of His Son. It is to take dominion in the earth and reveal His kingdom! We must recognize that His work in us brings us into the authority. Again, the Apostle Paul told the Ephesians we were His workmanship created in Christ Jesus unto good works.

Eph 2:10;

"For we are his workmanship, created in Christ Jesus unto good works, which God hath before ordained that we should walk in them"

We are ordained to walk in them. As those who are ordained to walk in the good works of Christ; we must have authority to advance the Kingdom of God as His representatives and ambassadors. Christ gave Himself to establish our place in Him; that we would be purveyors of His image and likeness.

Tit 2:14;

"Who gave himself for us, that he might redeem us from all iniquity, and purify unto himself a peculiar people, zealous of good works."

1Jo 4:17;

"Herein is our love made perfect, that we may have boldness in the day of judgment because as he is, so are we in this world."

We are as He is. Now there are many other aspects of this work of authority being established in the people of God. We do not have enough time to discuss them all in this book. Yet, in this order we understand there are implications here that relate to the Spirit Realm and our authority over the works of the adversary. Since Christ has defeated the enemy of our soul; His authority gives us the right and a mandate to destroy Satan's works and to take mastery over everything in creation. How awesome is the wisdom of God in Jesus Christ; to bring us as Sons of God, into His great glory! Authority reveals the grace of His Spirit and the Word given to us. It is absolute to His will being accomplished in and through the Body of Christ. The Body of Christ cannot and will not be able to carry out the responsibility given to it independent of its understanding of its Christ Authority. We must perceive the dimensions of this grace and its significance to the believer. Jesus remarked in:

John 5:26;

"For as the Father hath life in himself; so hath he given to the Son to have life in himself;

Christ is very focused in His understanding that He had the same authority as His Father. In the same thought we see this understanding being manifested in every dealing. When He confronted devils, He knew that He had authority to cast them out. He knew that He had authority to heal and to deliver from bondage. The crucial and most difficult part of our walking out the manifold wisdom of Christ; comes with our lack of insight into our authority as believers.

Philippians 2:6, tells us of the legitimacy of Christ's sonship, in this:

> *"Who, being in the form of God, thought it not robbery to be equal with God."*

So then the Church must not think it robbery to be equal with the Son of God as a condition of our covenant relationship with Him.

Joh 1:12;

> *"But as many as received him, to them gave he power to become the sons of God, even to them that believe on his name."*

We are Sons of the Father and joint heirs with Jesus Christ. We are *STANDARD BEARERS!* The Sons of God must stand up in the manifold wisdom of God!

CHAPTER THIRTEEN

"POWER"

Now Beloved, we have come to the 12th and final component in the foundation of the Standard Bearer. It is for all intents and purposes the place of God's greatest manifestation of His glory in Church. It speaks to the glory which is revealed in the POWER of God being displayed before men. God's ultimate objective is that of being glorified for His greatness and the works which display His power establish that end. David the King; continuously proclaimed:

Psalms 19:1;

"The heavens declare the glory of God; and the firmament shews his handiwork."

Ps 29:2;

"Give unto the LORD the glory due unto his name; worship the LORD in the beauty of holiness."

Ps 96:8;

"Give unto the LORD the glory due unto his name: bring an offering, and come into his courts."

Ps 145:11;

"They shall speak of the glory of thy kingdom, and talk of thy power."

All of these statements are very much insightful to the nature and the character of our God and the understanding He gives to His people regarding His power. His power is the ultimate revelation of His glory released in His kingdom.

Ps 104:31;

"The glory of the LORD shall endure for ever: the LORD shall rejoice in his works."

God's power will be realized within His works and the glory of God, recognized upon them as inseparable. We will come into the use and demonstration of the power of God as a part of the manifested glory of God in the Church. Now lets look at the types of power which are expressed in the working of God's will in believers. The very *First* is the Hebrew word *SARAH;* which means to prevail: or to have power as a prince. This is power which is given by station. Jacob held power with God as a prince in Israel.

Ge 32:28;

"And he said, Thy name shall be called no more Jacob, but Israel: for as a prince hast thou power with God and with men, and hast prevailed."

Ro 11:5;

"Even so then at this present time also there is a remnant according to the election of grace."

Ro 11:7;

"What then? Israel hath not obtained that which he seeketh for; but the election hath obtained it, and the rest were blinded."

We are positioned in Christ as those given specific station and assignment to the kingdom. There is no purpose of relationship which is not consistent with our position in Christ.

Eph 1:18;

"The eyes of your understanding being enlightened; that ye may know what is the hope of his calling, and what the riches of the glory of his inheritance in the saints,"

2Pe 1:10;

"Wherefore the rather, brethren, give diligence to make your calling and election sure: for if ye do these things, ye shall never fall:"

This is a charge of the Spirit of God and a condition of our position in Christ. Christ has called us and selected us for His glory. As those who are chosen for the express purposes of God; we are to give ourselves to the mandate of the Spirit. That is done in carrying out the instructions we receive through His Word. We are Kings and Priests and given a position that mandates the power of Christ, that the will of the Father can be accomplished.

Re 1:6; *"And hath made us kings and priests unto God and his Father; to him be glory and dominion for ever and ever. Amen"*

We are called to manifest the nature and character of Christ for the glory and praise of the Living God. The *Second* term for power is the Hebrew word KOACH which means:

be firm; vigor, literally (force, in a good or a bad sense) fruits, might, power(-ful), strength, substance, wealth. This is the power which speaks of force and ability to be firm and to produce. It is powerful, strength, substance, wealth, fruits and might.

It is given of God for productivity.

De 8:18;

"But thou shalt remember the LORD thy God: for it is he that giveth thee power to get wealth, that he may establish his covenant which he sware unto thy fathers, as it is this day."

Christ is positioning the Church (*Body of Christ*) to become fully productive in the earth. The initial command of God in the Garden of Eden was a mandate. Adam was the servant priest who would honor and bring glory to the Living Creator.

> Ge 1:28; *"And God blessed them, and God said unto them, Be fruitful, and multiply, and replenish the earth, and subdue it: and have dominion over the fish of the sea, and over the fowl of the air, and over every living thing that moveth upon the earth."*

After God destroyed every living thing in the earth during the flood; he again commanded Noah to be fruitful and multiply and to replenish the earth.

Ge 1:28;

> *"And God blessed them, and God said unto them, Be fruitful, and multiply, and replenish the earth, and subdue it: and have dominion over the fish of the sea, and over the fowl of the air, and over every living thing that moves upon the earth."*

So then we see that it is God who gives us the power to produce and be fruitful in the earth. Our Third word for power is the Greek word *EXOUSIA* meaning:

(in the sense of ability); privilege, i.e. (subjectively) force, capacity, competency, freedom, or (objectively) mastery (concretely, magistrate. It also means; delegated influence:--authority, jurisdiction, liberty, power, right, strength.

This word shows us that it is a privilege to use the power given to us by one in authority. Note that it is the same word used for *AUTHORITY*. Its influence is delegated. There can be no use of power without the delegated authority. Jesus spoke to the people concerning His delegated authority to use the power of the Father. He declares in

Mt 9:6;

> *"But that ye may know that the Son of man hath power on earth to forgive sins, (then saith he to the sick of the palsy,) Arise, take up thy bed, and go unto thine house."*

Then in the resurrection of Christ; we find that He delegates power to the Church.

Mr 16:17;

"And these signs shall follow them that believe; In my name shall they cast out devils; they shall speak with new tongues;"

Mr 16:18;

"They shall take up serpents; and if they drink any deadly thing, it shall not hurt them; they shall lay hands on the sick, and they shall recover."

The Body of Christ is given both authority and power to have dominion in the heaven's and the earth and under the earth. Yet, we find that the Body of Christ in many areas of its faith is impotent and lacks even the zeal and enthusiasm to exert pressure on the Word of God. The Word of God incites our faith (*faith comes by hearing*) and ignites our faith and brings potency to our authority.

Now the Fourth definition for power is found in the word *DUNAMIS*. It means;

force (literally or figuratively); specially, miraculous power (usually by implication, a miracle itself) y deed), (worker of) miracle(-s), power, strength, violence, mighty (wonderful) work.

It also has the dimension of violent and aggressive force which is required in the Spirit Realm along with persistence and momentum. This is the super spirit power of God which changes what is usual or normal to circumstances and conditions. It can be an acceleration of processes in the absence of time, i.e. if it normally takes six weeks to heal a broken leg; when dunamis power comes, it heals immediately. It heals miraculously. Dunamis works in conjunction with Kairos time. Kairos is the absence of time and it establishes instantaneous results. Because God operates outside of time; when He brings His presence upon the affairs of men, the results are instantaneous! This timelessness speaks to the glory of God's presence changing the dynamic of everything in creation. We must look for the presence of God with us to do the exceeding abundantly above all that we can ask or think. O' hallelujah to the matchless Christ and His wonderful power and glory! Now the final aspect of power is represented in the RESURRECTION of Jesus Christ. It is the most awesome and dynamic of all the power available to the people of God. This is power over death which is given to the believers. God has proven its value through Christ's death and rising again from the dead.

Ro 1:4;

> "And declared to be the Son of God with power, according to the spirit of holiness, by the resurrection from the dead:"

This is the power that will make the Body of Christ as a super spirit entity; most glorious in it's ministry. We can embrace the wisdom of The Lord Jesus Christ in becoming a visible display and evidence of the power of God in the earth. It will be such a remarkable demonstration that it literally changes the course of mankind. That course of change will show the magnanimous power of the Living God. This is the power made evident in the daily affairs of the world, as the Body of Christ goes forth in the earth to do the will of Christ. The Apostle Paul stated that his greatest longing was to know Christ. He further stipulated the conditions for knowing Him.

Php 3:10;

> "That I may know him, and the power of his resurrection, and the fellowship of his sufferings, being made conformable unto his death;"

This ultimate power in Christ is a standing up again, i.e.

(literally) a resurrection from death (individual, genitive case or by implication, (its author)), or (figuratively) a (moral) recovery (of spiritual truth):--raised to life again, resurrection, rise from the dead, that should rise, rising again.

The life of Jesus Christ is given to produce in us a moral recovery and standing up again that is complete. It will be realized in the manifestation of the Sons of God in becoming the image and likeness of Christ. This is the writing in the Word of God which says that Christ in us is the hope of glory!

Col 1:27;

"To whom God would make known what is the riches of the glory of this mystery among the Gentiles; which is Christ in you, the hope of glory."

Now it is time for the people of God to become conformed to the image and likeness of the Son of God! Come now, and let us bear His STANDARD!

CONCLUSION

What can we conclude from this teaching as we look back over the components we have been given. We find that everything that God the Father says and does is consistent with His nature and character. It is very necessary to recognize and to note that each component is built upon the one which precedes it. The foundations are set as evidence of the Apostolic dimensions of God's grace in making the Church His spiritual vanguard in the earth. We further acknowledge that what is in men's hearts are those things which speak to our daily living. They will be the Standard for measuring the truth of our success. God has nothing false or fallible to His character and it is because of His ability to work in our hearts and bring us conformed to His image and likeness that we have hope in Christ. Through becoming transformed to the image of His Son; we take on the nature of The Father and Son. We become HIS STANDARD BEARERS!

1Jo 4:17;

> *"Herein is our love made perfect, that we may have boldness in the day of judgment; because as he is, so are we in this world."*

When God our Father looks at us, He sees Jesus Christ as our finished end. We must allow the attributes of Christ to be formed in us and change us into true Sons of God by faith. Let us now review the twelve components again. Number 1 is *TIME*.

Ec 3:1;

"To every thing there is a season, and a time to every purpose under the heaven:"

Everything in creation is established upon time. If we do not recognize the TIMES; we will miss our seasons. What we do with time reveals what we value as important.

Number 2 is *COMMITMENT*. It takes commitment and understanding of time to live and fulfill our destiny.

1Pe 2:23;

"Who, when he was reviled, reviled not again; when he suffered, he threatened not; but committed himself to him that judgeth righteously:"

We will commit to what we spend time with. When we have an absence of time spent with what is of value or important; we lose commitment.

Number 3 is *AGREEMENT*. We cannot agree with what we are not committed to. It takes agreement to bring releases of power to our needs.

Mt 18:19;

"Again I say unto you, That if two of you shall agree on earth as touching any thing that they shall ask, it shall be done for them of my Father which is in heaven."

In this we understand that men will not agree with what they are not committed to. Agreement reveals our commitment.

Number 4 is *SUBMISSION*. Submission becomes a priority in allowing what we agree with to manifest in our living. We will not submit to what we cannot agree with.

1Co 16:6;

"That ye submit yourselves unto such, and to every one that helps with us, and labours."

Every believer is challenged with the issue of submission. Submission reveals the level of our agreement. What a man agrees with, he will submit to!

Number 5 is *OBEDIENCE.* **Men will not obey what they are not submitted to.**

Ro 5:19;

> *"For as by one man's disobedience many were made sinners, so by the obedience of one shall many be made righteous."*

Submission is established in obedience. When men are disobedient it is the evidence of the lack of submission.

Number 6 is *FAITHFULNESS.* **Men become faithful to what they obey.**

Mt 25:21;

> *"His lord said unto him, Well done, thou good and faithful servant: thou hast been faithful over a few things, I will make thee ruler over many things: enter thou into the joy of thy lord."*

We will distinguish our faithfulness by walking in obedience.

Number 7 is *RELATIONSHIP.* **Inside the nature of God, we learn to build relationship with the one we are faithful to and to whom we are faithful!**

Ga 6:6;

"Let him that is taught in the word communicate unto him that teacheth in all good things."

Php 4:14;

> *"Notwithstanding ye have well done, that ye did communicate with my affliction."*

Our relationship is an evidence of our faithfulness. The greater our faithfulness; the greater the relationship.

Number 8 is *FELLOWSHIP/COMMUNION*. When we build relationship, we can have fellowship together.

Php 1:4-5;

> *"Always in every prayer of mine for you all making request with joy, vs. 5 For your fellowship in the gospel from the first day until now;"*

When we build a relationship with Christ; we can have fellowship with HIM! The more we invest in relationship with HIM, the greater our fellowship becomes.

Number 9 is *UNITY*. Fellowship together, brings unity. Where we cannot have fellowship, we cannot have unity together.

Eph 4:3;

> *"Endeavouring to keep the unity of the Spirit, in the bond of peace"*

Fellowship and Communion will bring and establish Unity.

Joh 17:23;

> *"I in them, and thou in me, that they may be made perfect in one; and that the world may know that thou hast sent me, and hast loved them, as thou hast loved me."*

Number 10 is *ORDER*. Where there is Unity of Spirit, we have the Order of God. There is often limited order in the corporate Body of Christ because of lack of unity!

Col 2:5;

> *"For though I be absent in the flesh, yet am I with you in the spirit, joying and beholding your order, and the stedfastness of your faith in Christ."*

God sets Order and its is revealed in the Unity of the Believes

Number 11 is *AUTHORITY.* **God gives authority when He can behold our Order.**

1Co 16:1;

> *"Now concerning the collection for the saints, as I have given order to the churches of Galatia, even so do ye."*

The Apostle Paul tells them to do as he had instructed them. Therefore, Authority is always given. It can never be taken independent of the one who possesses it and has the right to give it. Order promotes Authority and Authority reveals the Order of God!

Mt 8:9;

> *"For I am a man under authority, having soldiers under me: and I say to this man, Go, and he goeth; and to another, Come, and he cometh; and to my servant, Do this, and he does it."*

God's Order is revealed in the Authority that is given.

Then finally Number 12 is *POWER.* **We have the right to exercise the authority that has been given. In the Body of Christ; the Lord will demonstrate the power He has given us in our everyday living. We will exercise the authority in the working of dynamic power and positional power through absolute dominion in the earth.**

> *"Lu 9:43; "And they were all amazed at the mighty power of God. But while they wondered every one at all things which Jesus did, he said unto his disciples,"*

> *Ro 1:16; "For I am not ashamed of the gospel of Christ: for it is the power of God unto salvation to every one that believeth; to the Jew first, and also to the Greek."*

God's power is revealed in the Authority that's given!

Let us walk then according to the measure of God's grace and the truth of His Word given to them that believe. We are His *STANDARD BEARERS* **in the earth and the salvation for all creation in Christ Jesus! AMEN!**

Printed in the United States
By Bookmasters